(NICHE)
and
Grow Rich

Practical Ways to
Turn Your Ideas Into a

BUSINE$$

Jennifer Basye Sander
and Peter Sander

Entrepreneur
Press

Editorial Director: Jere L. Calmes
Cover Design: Beth Hansen-Winter
Composition and production: Eliot House Productions

This publication is designed to provide accurate and authoritative information in regard to the subject matter covered. It is sold with the understanding
that the publisher is not engaged in rendering legal, accounting, or other professional services. If legal advice or other expert assistance is required, the
services of a competent professional person should be sought.

Library of Congress Cataloging-in-Publication Data
Sander, Jennifer Basye, 1958–.
Niche and grow rich: practical ways to turn your ideas into a busi-
ness/by Jennifer Basye Sander and Peter Sander.
p.   cm.
Includes bibliographical references.
ISBN 1-891984-76-4
1. Market segmentation. 2. Success in business. I. Sander, Peter. II.
Title.

HF5415.127 .S26 2003
658.1'1—dc21   2002040763

Printed in Canada

10 09 08 07 06 05 04 03   10 9 8 7 6 5 4 3 2 1

Table of Contents

Foreword

HAVING WORKED WITH JENNIFER AND PETER SANDER for the past year, I'm confident that you are about to embark on an enjoyable and information-packed journey in the pages of *Niche and Grow Rich.*

I set out several years ago to build a financial services business targeted towards a very large and strong niche—professional women. I knew from both my own experiences as well as marketing surveys that this was a powerful yet untapped niche when it came to financial services.

When meeting with potential investors I was able to clearly establish just who made up my niche market, why they needed this product, and how I planned to reach them.

Why do I believe so strongly in niche businesses? Because niche markets are profitable markets. Starting a business is a dynamic, courageous, and somewhat risky move. I believe that a well-considered niche provides a better chance of succeeding regardless of the business climate.

Many opportunities exist for entrepreneurs to discover untapped niches, primarily, but not only, through their own interests. Niche entrepreneurs must use creative and expansive thinking to identify niche, what it needs, and how to meet that need. Peter and Jennifer provide keen insight—and numerous examples—of good ideas and success stories built on market niches. But niche entrepreneurs must also think clearly and methodically, lest they run the risk missing the niche and coming up empty. Peter and Jennifer provide the framework to keep your idea generation on track through a successful business launch. This book stimulates your thinking but also structures your approach to creating a successful niche business.

Listen and learn from Jennifer and Peter.

—Jennifer Openshaw, founder of WFN.com
and host of PBS' "What's Your Net Worth?"

Introduction

FOR A SHORT TIME IN THE LATE '90s the path to business riches seemed dazzlingly simple—come up with a wacky scheme for an Internet business, get your college roommate to go in with you, call on a venture capitalist or two, and you're on your way! But just as quickly as it began, the bubble burst, sending many dotcom businesses down in flames and many still in the planning stages back to the drawing board.

Did the American dream of owning your own business and rocketing to riches disappear with the dotcom millionaires? Hardly. On every street in every town, and in almost every house on every block, sits someone with an entrepreneurial idea. With economic uncertainty and news of the high rate of failure associated with new businesses, every future business owner rightly asks the question: "What steps can I take to ensure that my business doesn't fail?"

The answer in many (if not most) cases is—find a profitable niche. Find a niche in which you can build your own unique stronghold, attracting, and maintaining customers who will pay top dollar for your goods or services. Find a niche in which you don't have to buy a multimillion dollar ad during the Super Bowl in the hope of attracting customers. In the right niche, your customers can easily be found in one place and can be accessed for little or no money. Find a niche where you don't have to look over your shoulder and worry about the competition. There isn't any competition, and you won't need to continually cut your prices.

Niche businesses are safe, long-term businesses. Niche businesses are promotable businesses. And niche businesses are *profitable* businesses.

How can *you* find an undiscovered niche, or determine whether the idea you already have will make it as a niche business? How does a concerned business owner find a niche and refocus the business towards profitability? These are all-important questions. As dedicated niche entrepreneurs ourselves, we—Jennifer and Peter—aim to answer them for you.

In the following chapters you will learn how to evaluate the profitability of a niche. Some niches are big and profitable, while others are small and profitable. There are some big niches that are not profitable. After reading *Niche and Grow Rich* you will learn to tell the difference *before* taking the plunge.

We'll begin with the basics—what exactly is a niche business? Why would you want to open a niche business? What are some examples of successful niche businesses, and why did they work? But more importantly—how can you discover a niche of your own?

You will soon learn where the best ideas come from, and how to let others do your market research for you. In her early 20s, co-author Jennifer Basye Sander's very first business was a niche business: a directory of woman-owned businesses. Did she come up with the idea herself? Heck no. She knew that both Los Angeles and San Francisco had successful directories just like it. Yet no one had done it in her hometown, the capital city of Sacramento. Armed with the knowledge that a similar business idea had worked twice before she was able to put the directory together quickly without too much financial risk, and reaped a great deal of financial reward. Once you learn this technique, you too will be hooked.

Not feeling creative? Don't worry. We'll share brainstorming techniques, research techniques, and other ways to find an idea. To keep you reading and believing that you, too, can pull this off, there are plenty of real-life examples of folks who have used these techniques to their advantage.

Are there any big trends that you should keep in mind when looking for a niche of your own? Yes. There is an entire chapter to address important trends and how they lend themselves to niche businesses. The possibilities are endless—what kinds of businesses can be successfully targeted towards aging boomers, adventurous travelers, or the small office/home office crowd? You'll be developing new ideas in no time.

Once you've found a niche, how can you make sure that it will sustain a business? Many start-ups have flopped because no one took the time to "do the due diligence" to make sure the niche was viable. Don't make this mistake. *Niche and Grow Rich* will help define niches, understand their needs, define products and services to meet those needs, and determine if a niche is large enough and profitable enough to justify an entire business.

You might not be ready yet to develop an entire niche business from scratch. A franchise with a niche market angle might be the way to go. Chapter 7 takes a look at the popular franchises that target niche markets.

Over the years we've talked to hundreds of would-be entrepreneurs, and the question that comes up the most is: How do I protect my ideas? If you do develop your own unique ideas into a business, there are legal aspects to be considered. Chapter 8 is critical with information on protecting unique ideas so you don't lose control of what is rightfully yours.

How can you get the word out about a business once you open your doors? There is a lot of strategy and information to share in Chapter 9 to help you acquire the basics of getting free publicity for your new niche business. One of the real pluses of owning a niche business is that they are often easier to publicize and market than other kinds of businesses. Imagine how easy it was for Jennifer to get free publicity for her *Sacramento Women's Yellow Pages*. It was much easier to get the local newspaper to write about her business directory of woman-owned businesses than it would have been if she were running yet another pizza business. Both authors are skilled marketers with hours of national television between them. Being written up in newspapers and magazines or getting on television is actually easier to pull of with a niche business, and we'll show you how.

Coming up with an idea for a business is fun. Running a business, on the other hand, is hard work. How do you build a business once you've discovered the right idea? Based on our own experiences and what other niche entrepreneurs shared, we've pulled together the basic steps to success in planning and starting a new niche business.

The next few hundred pages are filled with real-life stories and interviews with entrepreneurs. Planning a business can be a lonely pursuit, but you will recognize the traits and talents of like-minded entrepreneurs in the profiles that have been collected. You aren't the only one with high hopes and big dreams. Every successful niche business owner was once in the same spot you are now—at the beginning of a long journey. The journey can be perilous, rocky, frustrating, and sometimes quite frightening. But the entrepreneurial experience is also unlike anything you've ever done before. Take the journey. Join with us now in learning how to niche and grow rich.

Niche
What's That?

Y ou've been thinking long and hard about building a new business. That old nine-to-five job is stale, routine, and likely to go away soon. Standing in the shower every morning your mind drifts miles away into one of many "what if?" scenarios. What if I opened a restaurant? An outdoor furniture store? A day-care center? A cleaning service? Just as the image of you, CEO, flashes into your mind along with all the satisfaction that entails, the bubble bursts—how are you going to make money with other entrenched competitors waiting to pounce? The "what ifs"

*suddenly turn into "what if I can't make it?" "How can I pro-
tect myself against those big chains? The big box stores? The
big corporations? The entrenched little guys?" You turn off
the water, reach for a towel, and get ready for another hum-
drum day in the office....*

Ah, what a tempting book title. *Niche and Grow Rich*—how
could you pass it up? What, exactly, does that mean? Niche as a
verb? Niche to grow *rich*? What on earth are these two talking
about? Is there a way to build a business of your own that really
increases the chances for success? Guess what—*there is*.

There is a different way to think about business and markets.
Most people, when looking to establish a business, consider
things already done, and decide, "Well, I should get into that
business, too." They may have the skills and capital, and perhaps
there's room in the market for another player. But they will constantly be looking over their shoulders at their competitors, trying to out-price, out-advertise, and generally out-guess their
every move. What they do is dictated by what others do. They
fight on the same battlefield with all the other soldiers, vying for
advantage in what is a survival-of-the-fittest game. Can that
work? You bet—businesses can thrive on doing it better, and do it
all the time.

What we'd like to bring into the picture is the idea of doing it
differently. Play in an existing market, but take another approach.

Focus on a small, underserved piece of the market, and bring a unique, better product or service to it. Instead of fighting on the big battlefield, find a small hill, take it, and own it. Own that piece of ground. *Own that niche, and serve it well.* Get so good at it that your competitors won't bother you. If the competitor is a big corporation, maybe that "hill" is too small to be important to them. But it's not too small for you—in fact, it is big enough to make you, the entrepreneur, quite successful.

Read on for a complete tour and explanation of what a niche is, and how to identify one, and build a business to serve it. Then share our ideas—and those of many others—to learn all you can about finding and developing a niche business of your own.

Just What Is a "Niche"?

Let's get down to business and define just what the term *niche* means. It sounds like kind of a fancy French term (which it is). It sounds like it rhymes with *riche*, as in *nouveau riche* (which it does). And while the nouveau riche (the newly rich) are often made fun of, it is better to be nouveau riche than never riche at all!

The word niche brings to mind something small. Something manageable. A realm in which you can build your business and avoid many of the pitfalls waiting for any entrepreneur.

And so a niche business is…what, exactly? Simply stated, it is a business created to profitably serve the needs of a niche market. And doesn't that sound like where you want to be?

Why Niche?

What's so great about starting and running a niche business? Business is business, right? After talking with hundreds of business owners we've come up with some compelling reasons why you, too, should *niche and grow rich.*

❖ *You'll stand a great chance of succeeding.* Now that is a big claim to make. Why should a niche business be any likelier to succeed? Because you are positioning yourself as a bigger fish in a smaller pond. With that comes greater *market power* and with greater market power comes greater stability, pricing power, and profitability, and a more loyal customer base. You aren't as exposed to the whims of the economy, nor to those of the competition.

❖ *It will be easier to find customers.* Easier? Why? Because the tighter your niche, the better you will be able to capture customers, focus on their needs, and meet those needs. The customers you capture will be the right customers—ones you can do business with over and over again.

❖ *You'll have less competition.* A famous American general maintained that the secret to winning is to "get there firstest with the mostest." You'll be the first to serve your niche and should therefore capture the largest market share. Market leaders control markets so long as they preserve their advantage. They are the first to respond to trends, set the pace on product and service deployment, and set the terms on price. Isn't that where you want to be? You understand the market and lead the way in meeting its needs—creating what Warren Buffett would call a "moat" around your business and protecting it against competition as long as you stay in touch with your niche. Competition may happen, but you'll have a leg up, especially in the beginning.

❖ *You'll make more money.* Not only will you have more control over pricing and profit margins in your business, some operating expenses will be lower too. With a captive niche less will be spent for promotion and advertising to acquire new customers and preserve market share. Word-of-mouth is a powerful advertising tool in a well-defined niche.

❖ *You'll be able to do it over and over again.* Once you've built one successful niche business and understand the thought process behind it, what is to stop you from using that same knowledge to build a similar business that serves a slightly different niche? Or to add products and services to more profitably serve the existing niche? Such *crossover* niching works well—to identify new products and services to serve your existing niche or find new niches receptive to your current products and services. Online entrepreneur John Drummond and his wife, Amy, founded Unicycle.com, and quickly built a successful business shipping unicycles to customers around the world. "Now that I know how to build a Web site that caters to a specialized niche, I'm on the lookout for more ideas. Ideally I'd like to have five different niche Web sites, each pulling in a million dollars a year," says John. Maybe accident and health insurance is a good "crossover" product to introduce to the unicycle niche? More seriously, t-shirts, bumper stickers, and other "ephemera" would work, and who's to say unicycles couldn't "cross over" to the extreme sports, scooter, and skateboard crowd?

❖ *You won't be caught off guard by market changes.* In many niche businesses you are the perfect target customer; when your interest or needs shift or change, you'll know your customers will soon be shifting as well. Large corporations run from remote headquarters offices are the last to hear their customers have changed, defected, or otherwise moved on. But if you run a store for middle-aged surfers because you are a

WHERE DID THE WORD "NICHE" COME FROM?

*W*ebster's dictionary defines the word niche as "a recess in a wall, as for a statue." That image might help you visualize what you are trying to gain by developing a niche business. Imagine a large brick wall, each brick symbolizing a successful, well-funded business. Sometimes the business world can seem like that, can't it? It's like a solid and impenetrable wall that won't let you in. But then your eye lights upon a cozy little chink in the wall—a comfortable, inviting recess where the brick is set back a bit, allowing you a handhold, or sheltered place to sit during the rain. That could be your business—your own niche business. There in the solid wall of business you can carve out your own little nook. Peeling back another layer of meaning brings us to the French origin. The verb *nicher* means to nestle or rest. That sounds even cozier, doesn't it? Carve out your own niche business and nestle up inside, safe from the raging world of competition and cutthroat pricing.

middle-aged surfer who didn't feel comfortable buying in an atmosphere designed to appeal to young boys, you will be smack dab in the thick of things. And when your customers start looking for bright green shirts instead of pale yellow ones, you'll know it immediately. As a niche business owner, you will be nimble and swift. Just as in the example above, you will be able to quickly adapt to changes in your niche. A niche seller of ethnic cooking ingredients will be able to adapt much faster and more favorably than a supermarket to the latest cooking trends.

❖ *It is often easier to get financing for a niche business.* A lender who thinks you understand your market and are well positioned to serve it profitably is more likely to invest in you than another "me too" business and business plan.

From the Real World: Big Industry, Small Niche

Is there any point in trying to build a business in a large industry? If you can find the right niche inside a big industry or market you have a good chance of building a long-lasting and profitable business. Let's take a look at some huge industries, and how entrepreneurs have found a way to carve out a profitable niche without having to compete head-on with the industry giants.

> IF YOU CAN FIND THE RIGHT NICHE INSIDE A BIG INDUSTRY OR MARKET YOU HAVE A GOOD CHANCE OF BUILDING A LONG-LASTING AND PROFITABLE BUSINESS.

Soft Drinks

The minute you think of the soft-drink business two giants quickly come to mind: Coke and Pepsi. How could a smaller company possibly compete with these monoliths taking up all the market space? Why even try? Well, one spunky company in Colorado decided to build a soft-drink company with a new spin. Why not sell a bit of nostalgia, a soda that tastes like childhood, in a glass bottle that's a relic from the '60s? Now Cable Car Beverage Company owns the "classic soft drink" niche. Who knew there *was* such a niche until they created it? The Denver-based company first secured the rights to bottle Stewart's Root Beer from a chain of drive-ins in the East, and has now developed an entire line of classic soda flavors like Key Lime, Cream Soda, and Country Orange n' Cream. The niche paid off handsomely, and in 1997 they were bought by Cadbury Schweppes, which also owns Snapple.

Womens Retail Apparel

Once again, this is an industry with some enormous players and a sprawling, international market. How about starting a store that sells clothing to women and has to compete with big department stores and well-known name brands? It sounds like a nutty idea, unless you can find a way to make yourself different from what is already out there; or better yet, a need in the market no one else is addressing. Marvin and Helene Gralnick started the apparel chain Chico's FAS Inc. in the early '80s to fill a hole they'd spotted in the market: Who was selling clothes designed with middle-aged women in mind? Most mall stores catered to young girls and trendy styles. Who was serving well-heeled women who wanted to look good, but couldn't find figure-flattering, comfortable clothes? Marvin and Helene Gralnick began to produce a custom line of loose-fitting but stylish clothes for women in their 40s and beyond, available only in their own stores. It worked. Chico's FAS is now a publicly-traded company with more than 250 stores across the country.

Snack Food

You know Frito Lay, Nabisco, and Keebler. How about Granny B's Cookies of Orem, Utah, producers of "The Original Pink Frosted Cookie?" Oh, you haven't heard of them? Take a look in the nearest vending machine and you might spot a large pink-frosted cookie decorated with little sprinkles. Jennifer first bought one in a train station in Berkeley, California and loved its gooey frosting. She now buys them online at www.grannybs.com. Wes and Diane Homolik, founders of Granny B's, started out in the pizza business and sold the pink cookies (Diane's childhood creation) to their customers as dessert. Once they noticed how popular the cookies were, they got out of the pizza business and into the pink-frosted cookie business. Why pink frosting? "We've tried white, blue, and yellow, but it's the pink that does it," says Wes.

Fine Jewelry

Retail jewelry is a crowded, high-stakes, and competitive business. In almost every mall you will find not one, not two, but as many as a dozen storefronts from national jewelry chains. It seems unlikely that a successful niche could be found. But don't tell that to the Robbins family of Philadelphia. Decades ago they turned their jewelry store into an 8,500 square-foot establishment specializing in bridal jewelry—engagement rings, weddings bands, loose diamonds, and anniversary rings. All of their promotion and advertising is now targeted to that one niche—brides-to-be. Is it working? "We've dominated this market since we made the changeover in 1977," says Jason Robbins. In order to expand their reach even more, Jason built www.weddingband.com in 1994; it now receives a whopping five million hits a month thanks to advertisements in bridal magazines.

Television Broadcasting

Most parts of the TV market seem locked up by giant media players. But beginning in the 1980s with the spread of cable television, niche or speciality channels began to appear. Whereas viewers with an interest in history might have watched the occasional piece on public television, they seldom found prime-time network shows devoted to historical topics. Enter *The History Channel.*

Do you think it's important to keep up with what your elected representatives in Congress are doing? The major networks didn't, but the founder of C-Span did when he started a channel to cover that topic. Flipping through the hundreds of channels that exist nowadays is a great lesson in niche businesses. There are programs devoted to everything from gardening to crafts, with the merchandising to match.

Book Publishing

Romance novels are everywhere, from grocery stores to airport gift shops. But take a look at the swooning couples on the covers of most of them and you will notice they are a pale-skinned bunch. Wil Colom, the owner of Genesis Press in Columbus, Mississippi, founded a company to publish African-American romance novels after his wife complained she couldn't find any on the bookstore shelf.

Financial Services

After all the stock market hoopla in the last few years you know what a "discount broker" is, but do you also know it is a business niche created by one man—Charles Schwab? In the 1970s, the deregulation of commissions that brokerage houses charged their customers for stock transactions made it possible for Schwab to create an entire financial services company that offered something radically new. Never before had individual investors been able to pay a modest fee for a stock transaction with no large flat commission to a full-service house that provided all manner of "advice." Charles Schwab suspected there would be millions of small investors willing to skip the hand-holding and financial advice and place orders for stocks they chose themselves. He was right, and a new niche was born.

Hmmm....this makes sense. Take an existing market or business, and think of it differently. Enter it differently — through the side door, so to speak. Serve a unique market in a unique way. Capture those customers not served before. It can't spend billions building a brand or advertising or discounting the product, so this makes sense. Get a small piece of the market. Build a "moat" around the business by owning that piece of the market and serving it like no others can (or want to)....

2

Are You a Good Niche or a Bad Niche?

*S*itting in traffic, you turn the radio down and start thinking about that business again. A niche business. It's compelling, but scary. What if the niche isn't there? What if it's a flash in the pan? Big companies spend billions on such mistakes. NBC blew $100 million on the "XFL" believing it would serve the interests of a new, emerging group of young "extreme" fans. But they televised those games on Saturday nights, precisely when fans wished to be doing something else. Was it a marketing mistake or a mistake in execution? It doesn't matter. If NBC can blow it to *that tune, what's a little person like you doing thinking about niche markets? I'd better be clear on whether that niche is really a niche, or just a fad. On the other hand, didn't Starbucks start out serving a niche market...?*

Finding a niche sounds appealing, but is there such a thing as a bad one? Is it possible to misinterpret a need or market that looks appealing, but doesn't hold up to close scrutiny? Absolutely. The most challenging—and risky—part of establishing a niche business is correctly identifying and establishing the niche. If you think it's a lasting niche but it turns out to be a flash-in-the-pan fad, you will end up with nothing (or *less* than nothing if you borrow to start the business!). Identifying the niche is extremely critical and requires careful thought.

Remember the "big fish, small pond" analogy? It works. You don't want the pond to dry up, nor do you want it swamped by floods and competitive species. You want it to be there and stay as it is. When you've identified a pond that is well defined, stable, and big enough to supply the "food" you need, that's the pond you want. A niche is such an ideal "pond."

Terms: Niche, Fad, Trend, Lifestyle Change, Revolution

When is a niche a niche, and when is it not? Part of the "art" of setting up a niche business is being able to identify the niche, address its needs, and see its future. It's important to understand the characteristics of a niche "pond" and what distinguishes it from a broader market "sea"—or a fad market "puddle" that eventually dries up. A brief tour of terms will help.

- *Niche market* is a well-defined enduring market segment with common characteristics and specific needs; it is always present but often overlooked and underserved. Niches are consistent: they grow and fade only slowly over time if at all. One of the numerous examples covered here is snacks packaged specifically for airlines.

- *Fad market* is a market created by popularity, usually of a fad *product*, that rises rapidly in a short time and fades, either quickly or slowly. Examples include Pokemon (we *hope* it's just a fad!), wine coolers, and blush wines. A fad market may disappear or remain in existence; but it declines in size to a small fraction of its popularity apex.

- *Market trend* is an underlying *evolution* or change in habits, preferences, or tastes in response to lifestyle changes, priorities, demographic shifts, or a host of other phenomena. Trends often create or expand niche markets. For example, the gourmet coffee market so effectively captured by Starbucks arose in part from increases in disposable income, increasing distaste for public alcohol consumption and driving, expanding upscale and European conoisseurship, and an increase in individual entrepreneurs and homebased businesses. Having the right product at the right time with effective delivery sealed the success story. The niche may have always been there, but the trend built the niche into a recognizable, viable, and growing market.

- *Lifestyle changes* are wholesale trends, "run amuck" so to speak, that become more recognizable and work their way into larger segments of the population. One could say the

Starbucks phenomenon reflects a lifestyle change, where the café not only replaces alcohol, but becomes a meeting place, social hall, and business workplace for the masses. Lifestyle changes are bigger and more permanent than trends, and many start out as niche markets.

❖ *Revolution* is a once-in-a-while massive change in a marketplace usually brought on by a shift in technology or a major historic event. Markets change in "step function" mode and can create many new niches to be served. Compact discs became available in the early '80s and changed music distribution forever—providing a good opportunity for portable CD players, "jewel case" manufacturers, mail-order distributors, and distributors of music collections. It remains to be seen if the PC and the Internet are merely fads or a revolution, but they're probably the latter. And the CD revolution left a niche or two in its wake, such as the one that serves the needs of audio enthusiasts and collectors still sworn to vinyl LPs.

A Market Full of Niches

Some mainstream markets may be "solid walls" that lend themselves to few if any viable niches. It's hard to think of a market that has *no* niches, but some basic markets seem niche-resistant. Consider gasoline stations. There's not a lot of niche potential there, unless you own the only station at the airport or inside the national park, or wish to sell the high-octane stuff to old-car collectors.

A few markets behave more like a collection of niches. Take the audio electronics market; there are mainstream products from Japan Inc. in every consumer electronics superstore. But beyond these basic consumer entries there are dozens—hundreds—of specialty audio products for the more "enthusiastic" customer. There are all kinds of speakers, including West Coast sound, East Coast sound, compact, electrostatic, powered, and center subwoofers, from a potpourri of manufacturers. And don't forget the "little" stuff— "Monster" cables and other specialty cable systems that promise better sound through the correct alignment of conducting materials at the atomic level. There is everything from high-end $500 radios to $10,000 Mark Levinson amplifiers made of aircraft-grade components, to tube amplifiers for the enthusiast who likes to see the warm glow of light reflecting on the wall to accompany the pure, natural sound. And there are audio and "home theater" shops everywhere to allow the anxious listener to audition these products. All of these products and services came about by studying niches in the audio market and catering to those niches, which many of these companies have done successfully. But others have failed—especially in the speaker business—because the niches are too small or already occupied.

The point is that there are possible niches and niche businesses in almost any market, but some markets lend themselves more to niching that others. You must clearly identify your niche, product or service, and potential for a niche business.

Niche Market versus Small Market

You may ask, Isn't a niche market just a small market or subsegment of a larger one? Technically maybe, but there are defining characteristics of a niche that not only make it different but also much more effective to build a business upon. A niche market has a common set of needs and interests that one can build a set of products and services to serve. It is not just a small set of customers bounded by geography or demographics.

TABLE 2.1 Niche versus Small Market

Type of Market	Characteristics	Example
Niche market	• Specific customer needs	• Boat owners in a small coastal town
	• Concentrated customer base	• Old-time or classic soft drink market
	• Like demographic profiles	
	• Community behavior and common interests that can be served by a set of products and services	
	• No close substitutes	
Small market	• Diverse customer base and customer needs	• The population of a small coastal town
	• Close substitutes available	• Generic soft drink market
	• Little to no "community" or common denominator set of interests	

Dynamics of Trends, Fads, and Niches

Warning: looks can be deceiving. The $64,000 question to be answered by any prospective niche business owner or marketer is, Is it a niche or a fad? What appears to be a fad can turn out to be an

> WHAT CAN APPEAR TO BE A NICHE OR EVEN A TREND OR REVOLUTION CAN TURN OUT TO BE A FAD—AS IN ORDERING PET FOOD ONLINE.

DID SMOKE GET IN OUR EYES?

Take a look at what happened a few years ago in the cigar industry. Those of you who run cigar stores might want to skip ahead a few pages, rather than revisit what may have been a bleak existence.

Cigar smokers have been around for centuries. But in the early '90s cigar smoking suddenly surged in popularity, becoming a chic and trendy thing to do. Who didn't pick up and puff a cigar back then? Women smoked cigars, men smoked cigars; it was a part of every social gathering and the only way to celebrate a successful business deal or golf course outing. Whereas buying a cigar had previously been limited to a band of well-heeled men who sought out obscure shops, suddenly there were cigar stores on every corner, filled with comfortable leather chairs and smelling of high-end tobacco. Cigar bars, cigar accessories, Web sites, magazines, clothing—they all appeared. It seemed like a great niche to occupy, one in which all you had to do to make money was slap a cigar-themed logo on your product and watch the sales roll in.

Think about it now. When was the last time you (or a friend) smoked a cigar? A couple of years ago, right? Just as quickly as the fad appeared, it dissolved, leaving behind disappointed business owners who'd invested huge sums in cigar-related niche businesses. So what happened? Did cigar smokers disappear? Of course not. But their numbers have certainly diminished, and they are—once again—a niche market.

extremely lucrative niche. Starbucks is a good example. What appears to be a niche or even a trend or revolution can turn out to be a fad—as in ordering pet food online. To slightly modify a well-known saying, "God grant me the ability to recognize niches as they are, to accept the fads as fads, and the wisdom to know the difference."

To make it more interesting, realize that trends can give rise to niches, and niches can sometimes spark large and popular trends. Is your head spinning yet? The key to correctly identifying the niche lies in understanding the customer base that forms it and the unique products and services that can be delivered to it, and the underlying trends that are likely to support and build it in the long run. Customers, products, and trends: get that right, and you have a basis—once the numbers are run—for forming a business.

How can you tell the difference between a niche and a trend, particularly a trend that might disappear as quickly as it arrived on the scene? Is Pokemon a trend, fad, or niche? It's probably a fad, but children's trading card games are a niche and may become a resurgent trend similar to baseball cards in the '50s and '60s. Harry Potter is probably a fad, but magical and imaginative books for children are a niche and probable trend.

Are you getting the picture? A trend is an enduring shift in preferences and interests, while a fad is temporary. At the same time, a niche is a small stable segment of a market with like characteristics and needs that will rally around a certain well-defined set of products and services. A niche is not a fad, but may be built and supported by a market trend, or may in itself *be* the beginning of a trend. Minivans started out serving a niche market (families with small children) but spawned a trend towards lightweight, roomy trucks for everyone. Electric cars are a niche business, and remain so until the conditions are right to support an emerging trend. The

---

TENNIS, ANYONE?

Tennis provides a good example of the dynamics of niche markets, fads, trends, and even lifestyle changes. Do you remember tennis clothes and jogging suits? People—particularly midlifers—wore jogging suits everywhere. Tennis and other "jogging suit" athletics became a trend in the '70s and had earmarks of lifestyle change as midlifers suddenly went on an exercise kick. Parts of this trend were sustained and did became marketable lifestyle changes—served by health clubs, spas, and so forth. But for the poor purveyors of tennis equipment and wear, the apparent lifestyle change failed to give lasting lift, and alas, tennis is once again more of a niche market.

---

new VW beetle will probably turn out to be a fad—it won't go away completely, but will diminish in market strength and public mindshare.

This doesn't mean a niche business needs a trend or must spawn one to survive. Trends are nice for growth, but most niche businesses are quite comfortable serving a stable, consistent customer base and can do it quite profitably over a period of time. Many "niche" entrepreneurs look for the "crossover" opportunities to extend their business models to *other* niches, or create new products and services for *current* niches, to grow their businesses.

Niche Markets, Products, Marketing, and Businesses

Just when you think you've straightened out the differences between a niche, trend, and fad, here is another distinction to tackle.

Is there a difference between a niche business, a niche market, niche product, or niche marketing? You might hear the terms used interchangeably, but we believe there is a difference. Let's take a look at each term.

Niche Market

A niche market is a small segment of a larger market with common needs and interests. Airline travelers are a large market, but corporate officers and high-level business executives form a niche within that market. The pet market is huge, but owners of ferrets would "ferret out" a tiny niche segment not served by most firms in the business.

Niche Product

A niche product *is a specialized product or service created specifically to serve the needs of a niche market.* It is often a specialized portion of a broader product or product line. Snacks packaged for air travel would be a niche product made by a snack goods packager, as are laundromat-sized detergent boxes for a detergent manufacturer. The book title *Microsoft Office '97 for Law Firms* is also a good example of a general product with a specialized twist to serve a niche market. Niche products can be further classified into *physical products, niche services, niche distribution, and niche locations.*

- ❖ Niche *physical products* are specially created products or packages for certain niche markets. Examples include large-type books, airline snacks, and maternity clothes.
- ❖ Niche *services* are ones where the product is really the service. Home grocery delivery for busy professionals is an obvious example. Special knowledge or expertise can also be a "service" that helps define the niche—as in expertise on

Amazon parrots supporting a specialized bird or bird supply business in that niche.

❖ Niche *distribution* is where the "value add" is concentrating a set of existing products to serve a particular market. This is likely to occur on the Internet. For instance, Gazoontite.com markets equipment to relieve allergy sufferers; Camera world.com offers photographic equipment and supplies to the photo enthusiast; and 1-800-Batteries carries any kind of battery you might ever need. Often value-added education and how-to services are bundled in with the concentrated distribution.

❖ Niche *location* is where a common product or service is delivered on-location to the specialized niche at that location. The location defines the niche. Suntan lotion at the beach, oil changes in company parking lots, and flowers sold in restaurants are all examples.

Niche Marketing

Niche marketing is a strategy or campaign that markets a broad product or product line to a specific niche. For example, United Airlines might learn the needs of gays, then target ad campaigns

A NICHE MARKET IS A SMALL SEGMENT OF A LARGER MARKET WITH COMMON NEEDS AND INTERESTS. A NICHE PRODUCT IS A SPECIALIZED PRODUCT OR SERVICE CREATED SPECIFICALLY TO SERVE THE NEEDS OF A NICHE MARKET. NICHE PRODUCTS AND MARKETS CAN BE DEFINED BY PHYSICAL PRODUCT, SERVICES, DISTRIBUTION, AND/OR PHYSICAL LOCATION.

THINK SPEED

As you ponder your niche business opportunities, think *speed*! Many a niche business has been founded on the idea not of doing something new, but of doing something fast! To take a common product or service and deliver it faster than normal—absolutely, positively overnight—makes for an effective business strategy and value proposition (see Chapter 6). Of course, the classic example is Federal Express. Sure, small package delivery existed with the U.S. Postal Service and their brown-trucked competitors before Fred Smith came along and carved out the overnight niche (with the help of several marketing and operational innovations to support the idea).

You can do this, too. Through a bit of Cincinnati-bred hustle and special arrangements with suppliers, Dave Brown Commercial Photography of Cincinnati can deliver a fully processed professional photo using traditional photographic processes in two days; using high-end digital equipment it is same day. This beats the normal one-to-two week wait when the customer is trying to get an important marketing piece out the door. Not only does it define the niche, it also allows the firm to charge more for the same product. It's a classic win-win—customers with a special need get special service, while the business prospers on higher revenue and less competition. Once you establish that dependability and quality go hand in hand with speed, customers are yours forever—and will gladly tell others where to get things done quickly.

towards this lucrative market. They might go so far as to "tweak" their existing product base to offer a variation for this customer niche (gay companion tickets at reduced prices). United would be doing niche marketing, but would hardly be considered a niche *business*. Do you see the difference? Niche marketing is a *technique* used by large businesses to increase their business by focusing on smaller niche markets.

Niche Business

A niche business is one built entirely to serve a niche market. It may deliver a niche product to that market, or it may deliver a standard product but add value by focused promotion, pricing, or distribution.

As you explore options and begin to build out your business idea, it is crucial to understand the relationship between niche markets, niche products, niche marketing, and your ultimate goal—a niche business. If you're starting from scratch, the path of least resistance is to start a niche business. If you're already in business, adding niche products or focusing on niche markets using "niche marketing" may be the path to success. As in all marketing—and all business—you *need to be clear on what you're doing* and *why*.

AS YOU EXPLORE OPTIONS AND BEGIN TO BUILD OUT YOUR BUSINESS IDEA, IT IS CRUCIAL TO UNDERSTAND THE RELATIONSHIP BETWEEN NICHE MARKETS, NICHE PRODUCTS, NICHE MARKETING AND YOUR ULTIMATE GOAL—A NICHE BUSINESS.

We continue to believe that the best way to niche and grow rich is to build a niche business that markets a good, needed product or service to a well-defined niche audience. Don't try to take on an entire market—it costs too much to get started and the competitive sharks will circle well before the first signs of blood appear. If you're already in business, think niche products and markets; if you're in a *niche* business, think *crossover* to other niche markets or products and services for your existing niche.

Finding Your Niche

Finding a niche business, especially one that (a) works and (b) fits your skills and interests can be a challenge. It takes observation, an open, creative mind, and a realistic business assessment. Look, think, and analyze. A common misperception is that you have to be *part of* the niche to make it work. True, it *helps* to understand the market, customer needs, and products if you are part of the niche; large-chested women may have a slight edge in creating a large-sized bra store for other "large" women. And if you deal directly with customers, it helps in establishing rapport. But it is by no means a *requirement*. As long as you *understand* customer needs, it hardly matters whether you are a customer yourself.

Outside the Box

Niche businesses arise out of flexible, sideways, outside-the-box thinking. Straight-line thinkers have a harder time hitting the mark. If you want to open an ordinary computer dealership, you're probably doomed to failure. Large and online retailers and a field full of smaller ones will eat your lunch unless you bring something special to the market. How about selling computers—and connectivity and training—to the over-65 group? They have the money (many of them, anyway) and the need to communicate (e-mail their families) and buy online (it saves trips to the store). Microsoft products are even more foreign to them than to the rest of us. This is a market with specific needs, from specialized setup and training to configurations for large font monitors and print. Learn the needs, create the services and perhaps physical products, and target the market, and you may have a viable business. (Of course, run the numbers first; you'll learn more about that later.) As an example, check out SeniorSurfers.com, a computer training and services business set up and aimed squarely at the seniors market. Another example is Premier Computer Systems of Sacramento, California, which sells PCs that aren't sold in stores—notably Dell. There is a market for people that want a Dell computer but want to see it, touch it, and get local support. In the "doesn't hurt to ask" department, Premier asked for—and got—contractual status as a Dell retail outlet, and is the only one in the country. Think sideways, backwards, and outside-in about your customers and how they're served in the marketplace, and you're bound to come up with a good niche concept.

Niche by Accident

Sometimes a niche business happens completely by accident. Happy industrial accidents occur all the time, and produce useful things like Teflon® and Post-It® notes. Can it happen to you?

> THINK SIDEWAYS, BACKWARDS, AND OUTSIDE-IN ABOUT YOUR CUSTOMERS AND HOW THEY'RE SERVED IN THE MARKETPLACE, AND YOU'RE BOUND TO COME UP WITH A GOOD NICHE CONCEPT.

One ambitious entrepreneur worked long and hard to set up a large-scale office paper recycling operation, only to find that the big companies he'd hoped to service were concerned about the sensitivity of their paper. Overnight a secure paper shredding business was born. Be forewarned—good business people seldom wait for accidents to happen.

A Blinding Flash of the Obvious

Sometimes the best niche is right under your nose. It may be that the one for you is in the industry you've worked in for many years. Rather than trying to start a business and learn from scratch in a new area or industry, why not look more closely at what is going on around you?

> RATHER THAN TRYING TO START A BUSINESS AND LEARN FROM SCRATCH IN A NEW AREA OR INDUSTRY, LOOK MORE CLOSELY AT WHAT IS GOING ON AROUND YOU.

Suppose you've been working in the printing industry for many years, but now have a hankering to strike out on your own. Instead of opening a pizza delivery business or lawn maintenance service, why not put all of your years of experience, contacts, and knowledge to work in trying to develop a niche business that serves other printers?

You can use this thought process regardless of the industry you are in. Start out by thinking about your career. What kinds of products or services do you wish existed to help you do your job? Expand your business search to include your colleagues and even your competitors. Ask them the same question: What does this industry need? Sometimes the right niche answer develops naturally as you slowly notice a need that could be filled.

Laurie Rood entered the insurance industry out of college; she'd heard it was a place women could make great money. After seven years of working as an agent and a broker, Laurie began to develop a specialty in employee benefits. After her zillionth phone call in which she had to patiently and clearly explain a benefits package to a confused employee of a large corporation, a light went on in her head. "I realized that there was a tremendous need for someone to explain benefits to employees. So much of what they received in their benefits package from their employer was not only laden with industry jargon, but pretty dull and complicated as well." Laurie's company, Rood & Dax Advanced Insurance Services, now specializes in designing and developing brochures that make it easy for an employee to understand their benefits. Is this the sort of great business idea that would come to you late at night? Not unless you'd been inside the industry for years and witnessed an unanswered need.

If you want to understand someone, walk a mile in their shoes. Remember that expression? What if you'd walked a mile in large, floppy clown shoes? You'd definitely understand the clothing needs of fellow clowns. Tricia Bothun was a clown with Ringling Brothers Barnum & Bailey Circus and also performed on her own. Over the years she found herself drawn more and more towards designing the costumes for clowns rather than performing, and finally founded her own custom design company, Priscilla Mouseburger Originals in Maple Lake, Minnesota. She knew the market for clown costumes existed because she herself had been a clown on the lookout for the right outfit. She was a clown first, and a clown costume designer second. Tricia knew from her years of clowning that a great costume can make all the difference in your performance. "When clowns feel good about themselves, they're more likely to jump to a new level of creativity as a performer," she points out.

Keeping an eye out for new niches doesn't stop once you've established your business. The more involved you get with your industry, the more you'll spot new and unique ways to capitalize on niches, or create your own.

What could be new about sushi? How can you possibly do something different with raw fish and rice? Well, you could try to sell it to basketball fans. Who would have thought just a few short years ago that fans of the NBA team the Sacramento Kings would one day be cheering their players on with one hand, and holding a California roll in the other? A Sacramento-based sushi chain called Mikuni is doing just that. But Mikuni co-owner Derek Fong thought he could do even more with sushi. Surely there was another niche they were missing, some new way to extend the popularity of drinking saki and eating raw fish. He began to investigate what others in the industry were doing in order to build their businesses. What were they all missing? What about sushi that... moves? Meet the Mikuni Sushi Bus. "No one else was doing anything like it," Fong notes. The bus rents out for private parties for $150 an hour, plus the cost of the food and liquor, and has met with immediate success for birthdays, corporate events, and fundraisers.

By now we hope you understand the above terms and concepts and are beginning to see the advantages of operating a niche business. The last few pages gave you a sense of how niche businesses can grow out of the understanding of a marketplace. But what if you aren't that thrilled with the marketplace or profession you are in? What if you want to make a radical shift and develop a niche business totally unlike what you do now? Read Chapter 3 and learn how you can start to develop idea after idea until you finally find the one that is right for you.

Summary for Chapter 2

* ❖ There are many *reasons* to niche: It is easier to connect with customers and get backing, there is less competition, and there are higher profits.

* ❖ A *niche market* is a well-defined, enduring market segment with common characteristics and specific needs; it is always present but often overlooked and underserved.

* ❖ Niche markets *differ* from fads, trends, lifestyle changes, and revolutions. But niche markets can often profit from—or evolve into—trends, lifestyle changes, and revolutions.

* ❖ Niche markets are identified by *needs*—not demographics.

* ❖ Niche products include physical *products, services, location,* and *distribution.*

* ❖ A *niche business* serves a *niche market.* Larger businesses may also do *niche marketing* to serve a niche market.

* ❖ Finding and serving niche markets requires creative, "outside the box" thinking about customers and markets.

Aha! Now I'm starting to get it! A niche market opportunity can be a different approach to an existing business! Starbucks may be a different approach to the corner bar, with the added benefit of serving a larger market (under 21), being cool with a great product, and serving millions of new independent "free-agent" workers looking for a home away from home. That's complex. But I can also keep it simple. I could deliver the same professional photographs as anyone else — but do it overnight for stressed, last-minute marketing campaign managers. Or I could deliver really good food at sporting events, instead of lousy hot dogs and popcorn. Hmm....

3

Finding a
Good Idea

E very day in the shower, and sometimes at four in the morning, this niche thing keeps crawling into my brain. There's gotta be a niche out there just waiting for me. There are so many possibilities; I just need to lock in on the right one, and get a business going. But there are hundreds — thousands — of ideas. Some are completely new; some are new twists on an old business. Heck — maybe I can copy a niche idea someone else has had, and just do it in my neighborhood. How do I generate niche ideas, and start narrowing down the possibilities to those critical few that may be worth a go?

Okay, you've decided. You DO want a business of your own; one in which you call the shots, and better yet, reap the profits of your own hard work. But wait: Before you start a business, you must have one critical thing—a workable idea. Must it be unique in order to be successful? Absolutely not.

As a young entrepreneur of 23, Jennifer received a great deal of local press and media attention for a brilliant idea—a business directory that listed local businesses and professional services owned and operated by women. At the celebration launch party she even got a gold-embossed congratulatory letter from the Governor of California, lauding her for her valuable contributions and calling it "a wonderful achievement." It was heady stuff for a girl just a few years out of college. Even better, *The Sacramento Women's Yellow Pages* was a sales sensation.

But was it actually *her* idea? Did Jennifer wake up one morning in her apartment in Sacramento and think, Hey, what this world needs is a directory of woman-owned businesses? No, that's not the way it happened. It was more like this: One morning she woke up and thought, I sure hate working in politics, what else can I do? She remembered that in college she'd bought a copy of a little directory of woman-owned businesses in the San Francisco Bay Area. Hmmm,... she thought, I wonder if that same idea would work in Sacramento? It did.

Owning a business of one's own is an attractive idea to millions of Americans. But coming up with a workable idea is a skill in and of itself, one that not every would-be entrepreneur is lucky enough to be born with. Jennifer isn't the only entrepreneur who let someone else do her test marketing for her. There are many great examples in the big business world. In the early '70s a San Diego man and his sons built a company called The Price Club; it was the first-ever discount shopping warehouse. It wasn't long before similar businesses sprang up around the country under the names Sam's Club and Costco. When your business is a success, *everybody* pays attention.

In 1983, at the same time that Jennifer was successfully selling advertising and compiling information for her business directory, a friend approached her with a business proposition. "Fresh roasted coffee is going to be huge," he predicted. "It is all the rage in San Francisco and Berkeley, but no one is doing it here yet. Let's get together a group of investors and start a roasting company." A group of friends, including Jennifer, did get together in Sacramento that year, and they did start a coffee roasting company. Almost 20 years (and several partnerships) later, the Java City coffee company has a huge presence throughout the northern California region. If Jennifer had been smart enough then to trademark her "Jennifer's Blend" specialty roast (which became Java City's House Blend), her life would be vastly different. Imagine what just a half-cent royalty per cup on millions and millions of cups would have paid.... Ah well, you'll learn more about preventing that potential pitfall in Chapter 8 on trademarks and copyright.

Are you ready to start generating money-making ideas? Let's go!

The Idea Factory

Welcome to The Idea Factory, where you'll get your creative gears moving and flexing and begin to look at the world in a whole new way. You will soon turn into a 24-hour idea machine, trained to scan the landscape looking for new and profitable ideas. Are you ready? Then open the big heavy doors of this factory and come on in....

There are three categories of ways to get you brainstorming about niche businesses. Don't forget to keep a pad of paper and a pencil nearby; you will soon find yourself making notes as the new niche ideas start to form.

Update an Old Idea

The idea of "business" has been around for thousands of years. Whether it was a farmer bartering his wheat for milk from his neighbor's cow, or someone renting out a spare room, people exchanging goods and services for money is an age-old idea. Since business began, a good many different types of goods and services have been created. Some of them you are familiar with; some you are not. And it may be that a workable niche business can be found by updating an old idea and putting a new and modern spin on it. Does this sound far-fetched? It's not. Take a look at these examples:

Swift Horses... Swift Planes. When the American West was first being settled, a service was organized using swift horses and riders to deliver information to people as quickly as possible. Sure, you read about it in grade school; it was called the Pony Express. Although it looms large in our childhood imaginations, it operated for only a few years before becoming obsolete. And who needs horses delivering anything nowadays? Well, think about the business model that Fred Smith used to develop Federal Express: Isn't it just an updated version of the Pony Express? It's like the Pony Express with planes. Maybe Fred's idea came to him one afternoon in grade school, instead of at Harvard Business School.

Here's the Delivery Boy. Many of you have heard from your parents about how when they were kids the neighborhood grocer used to send a delivery boy around with the family purchases.

Grandmother just phoned the store and read a list of what she wanted: flour, eggs, sugar, and a sack of potatoes. There wasn't that much choice; most food was fresh, so she never worried about which brand to order. But then prepackaged foods were developed, big grocery stores appeared, and delivery services vanished along with the little guys who owned the stores. That is until Webvan tried to update the idea with their online grocery store and delivery service. Oh, you don't think Webvan is a good example since it failed so publicly? Similar services have worked on smaller scales; however, Webvan tried to do it all at once. Unfortunately, the niche, while clearly there, wasn't large enough to create the scale necessary to support the business model. This is one of the biggest dangers in setting up a niche business. Chapter 6 takes a closer look at niche size and determining the viability of a niche business.

Coffee House Transformation. Howard Schultz worked for a small Seattle coffee company and made frequent trips to Europe. Sitting around cafes has been a habit of Italians for generations, and Howard was happy to partake of the local tradition. As he explains in his business autobiography, *Pour Your Heart Into It*, he began to wonder if maybe, just maybe, this same café concept could catch on in Seattle. What if Starbucks, the company he worked for (and later bought), began to build cafés filled with comfy chairs and couches? Would it work? Would busy on-the-go Americans stop what they were doing and sit in a café with a cup of coffee for half an hour? You know the answer to that one!

Freshly Brewed. Dip back into European history once again and picture those scruffy old taverns where each individual owner had his own fiercely guarded secret recipe for ale and attracted devoted crowds with the specialty taste. Long a mainstay in the market-place, these taverns disappeared with the rise of big manufacturers and distributors. Beginning in America in the early '80s though, devoted home brewers began to open restaurants where their own brews were the star attraction; they also started small one-beer breweries all over the country that only served a small regional area. In Boulder, Colorado you can drink the house brew at the Oasis Brewery; in Sacramento, California, it's The Rubicon. Today's microbreweries are a classic case of how to successfully dust off an old business idea and reintroduce it to a niche market.

Ask yourself, Is there a business that used to exist and doesn't any longer? Is there a way you can update an old idea, put a spin on it, and roll it out to a newer, fresher audience? Ask your folks if there is a business or service they remember from their childhood that could be dusted off and reintroduced. Okay, so maybe the world doesn't need many wagon-wheel repair shops or buggy whip manufacturers anymore, but what about some of the old artisan skills? A great niche business would be to gather up a group of craftsmen with old-world skills like mural painting and wood carving. Form a high-end craftsmen's guild and market your group to interior decorators and architects of expensive homes. Are you getting the idea? It is still possible to reach back into history and extract an idea that will work for today.

Find Something that Has Worked Somewhere Else

Howard Schultz of Starbucks brought a tradition from Italy—sitting around for hours in a café sipping coffee drinks—and gave it an American spin. But what about ideas like Jennifer's women's business directory? These are ones that have been successfully introduced in a region but are just waiting for you to discover and introduce them successfully in your part of the country!

Before Jennifer began to compile *The Sacramento Women's Yellow Pages*, or sold one single ad or got a printing bid, she knew the concept had been successful in the San Francisco Bay Area; she'd also read about a similar project in Los Angeles. It was the early '80s and professional women were ready to embrace the idea of supporting other female business owners. The idea seems stale now that woman-owned businesses are so common. But back then it was unique, and Jennifer believed that she, too, could put together a business directory and make it work. So, on your own travels around the country, consider what you have observed in one place that hasn't yet been introduced to your area.

The next time you visit a new place, keep your eyes open as you drive down the street. Read the local business section with particular interest. Ask the locals what's new and what's working. You just might stumble across the perfect niche business.

When you relocate to a new area, look around to see what's missing. Maybe your favorite type of business, the very one you used to frequent yourself, hasn't yet arrived in this new place. Were your Saturday mornings spent hanging out at the local international newsstand, thumbing through issues of *Le Monde*, and catching up on what was going on around the world? The patrons of Newsbeat, in the college town of Davis, California, have spent many a morning that way. But hey, your new town doesn't have a place like that... so maybe you should start it. Or perhaps you always spent your Saturday mornings rummaging through the ever-changing booths at the local antiques co-operative, trying to find the last few pieces of a china pattern you collect. Oh, there isn't an antiques co-op in your new town? Bingo.

The Kopi Café in Chicago is a coffee house with a twist—an emphasis on international travel. Not only can you get a cup of coffee and a slice of sinfully rich chocolate cake, you can also buy a map and guidebook for whatever far-flung destination you are planning to visit. And you can buy small travel accessories like blank journals, passport holders, or money belts. The café itself is decorated with an international flair; masks and woven cloth hangings from around the world adorn the walls, along with postcards sent back to the café from patrons wandering from country to country. These elements all combine to make a coffee house that is distinct and different from all those around it. Would it work in your town?

Or, more cannily, if you are jealous of a particularly successful business already in your area, why not move somewhere it doesn't yet exist and establish one yourself? Jennifer remembers that in the early days of American River Roasters, the coffee company she helped start, several of their own patrons were so intrigued by the idea of roasting coffee (and that they could make a profit on it) that they went off to start roasting companies in outlying areas of Sacramento.

Does every niche business idea travel well? The short answer is "No." You'll have to put aside your own passionate feelings for the product or service and examine it from a practical business standpoint. You'll find the formula for how to do that in Chapter 6. In the meantime, take a look at two examples from our own family files; they are niche businesses we love, but ones we know wouldn't make the move to our town of Sacramento intact.

A Bowl of Red. Peter is from Cincinnati, and a big fan of the local chili style—a slightly sweet and Mediterranean flavor developed by

Greek immigrants in the late '40s. On almost every street corner you'll find a parlor that serves this special chili with spaghetti, sprinkled cheese, kidney beans, and raw onions in a short-order restaurant format. For years Peter has been after Jennifer to give it a try in Sacramento, but she is not convinced the unusual regional flavor would catch on.

LISTEN UP!

As a child you were taught not to listen to other people's conversations... or at least not to get caught doing it. Now we think you should listen in; but please do it discreetly. Eavesdropping can be a profitable endeavor if you use it as part of your idea-generation plan.

What is it you should be listening for? Listen in a store for what people are requesting—is it something you could produce? Listen at a party to what people are complaining about—is it something you could provide a solution to? A famous tale of how to profit by listening in comes from the book world. About ten years ago a publisher was browsing near the computer book section and overheard an exchange between a customer and a clerk. The customer asked for a book on DOS, and the clerk showed him a few selections, all of which looked overwhelming for the beginner. "No. What I need is something like DOS for dummies," the customer explained. DOS for dummies, the publisher thought to himself; not a bad title for a book. That day a 100-million-copy book series was born.

Swedish Delights. On North Clark Street in Chicago (across the street from the Kopi Café), you'll find Wikstrom's, a charming small grocery store that specializes in Swedish foods and packaged items. Jennifer stocks up there yearly on Swedish pancake mix and special cheeses, and wishes this tiny store was closer to her California home. Would this successful niche business thrive in her Granite Bay neighborhood? No. North Clark Street runs through an old Chicago neighborhood with a big Scandinavian population, and all of those folks shop at Wikstrom's for a taste of the old country. It's a great niche business, but it will only work well right where it is.

Refocus a Big Idea Towards a Specialized Market

Another way to generate ideas for niche businesses is to break off a small piece of a big market and refocus it to a different audience. Frozen TV dinners, those little aluminum trays with frozen dollops of mashed potatoes and gravy, applesauce, sliced turkey, and corn have been a part of American life since the '50s. Admit it: you eat them, too. Are they healthy, though? Is it a good idea for us to be feeding these frozen meals to our children?

Fran Lent worked for ten years in the consumer packaged food industry, and came to believe she'd spotted a hole in the market. As the working mother of two young children she was often too busy to cook, but didn't feel great about feeding her children fast food or frozen dinners. Drawing on her knowledge of the industry, Fran developed Fran's Healthy Helpings—a line of nutritious frozen foods for children. In 1995 she quit her job and invested her savings in kid's meals with names like Soccer-oni & Cheese and Twinkle Star Fish. Now that she's carved off her own piece of the frozen

ANOTHER WAY TO GENERATE NICHE BUSINESS IDEAS IS TO BREAK OFF A SMALL PIECE OF A BIG MARKET AND REFOCUS IT TO A DIFFERENT AUDIENCE.

industry pie, you can find Fran's Healthy Helpings on the shelves in major stores like Wal-Mart and Kroger.

The food industry isn't the only one in which you can refocus a big idea and aim it towards a niche. A recent Reuters news article focused on a new niche in the underwear business. Thongs, you're thinking? No, the newest business trend is sexy, lacy bras for big-breasted women. It seems that this niche has long been ignored in the lingerie business. Most companies made only plain, off-white, thick-strapped, and serviceable bras for big women. So within a large category (the underwear business) there is now a small niche (pretty bras in big sizes). Why not go one step further and create an entire store that focuses on these items? Call it Big Sexy Women. Sounds like a hit!

The travel agency industry is huge and dominated by large chains like American Express and Carlson Wagonlit. How is a little travel agent going to survive? Laurie Battiston, the owner of Uniglobe Expert Travel in Covington, Kentucky, knew she needed to find her own niche in which to specialize. A successful afternoon behind a booth at a local bridal show gave her an idea: Why not focus strictly on honeymooners? That's what she did, and it worked. Trips to Bermuda, Hawaii, and Mexico sell to newlyweds month after month. Once again, this is a big category (travel agencies) in which a canny business person carved out their own small niche (selling trips to honeymooners). Another travel agent who has found a profitable niche is Helena Koenig of Chevy Chase, Maryland. She started a company called Grandtravel in the late '80s to offer national and international trips to grandparents traveling with their grandchildren. What's the most popular trip of all? A safari to Kenya.

What If.... How can you put this technique to work? Read anything you can about big business—in *The Wall Street Journal, USA Today, The New York Times*. Whenever you run across an item that interests you, take a hard look at that category and ask yourself, What if I put a different spin on this? What if I took a similar business/product/ service and tweaked it just a bit to make it more luxurious/smaller/ streamlined/special for a different customer or niche audience?

THE SWEET SOUND OF SUCCESS

Connie Hallquist loved her grandmother Rose, but was always at a loss when it came to gift giving. "For years I gave her smoked salmon, or assorted jams and teas. I lacked any originality. What I really wanted to give her was something stylish, yet practical. Something she could use as her health failed, but that didn't look like it came out of a medical supply catalog." What Connie ended up doing was buying a plain cane, and then decorating it herself. Her grandmother loved it, as did her friends. And Connie began to wonder, Is there a business here?

Connie's own background was in business consulting, and she worked with clients like Williams Sonoma, Audi, and Levi Strauss.

She was no stranger to the idea of forming a business targeted to a specialized market. Once the idea for a company that targeted stylish senior citizens formed, Connie worked up a business plan. "Nobody was taking advantage of this category when I was doing my business plan in 1993, no one with any sense of style." Then Connie's own career plans changed, and she took a job transfer to England and reluctantly put her business plan aside.

Returning to the United States several years later, Connie saw that this category was still not being served. She successfully sought funding from Brand Farm Inc., and in the spring of 2000 launched Gold Violin as both a catalog and Web site.

So we asked, Has she managed to niche and grow rich? "From your mouth to God's ear," she laughed. "But I am on the verge of opening my first retail outlet." The first Gold Violin store will be near her company headquarters in Charlottesville, Virginia. Oddly enough, it will also be near a large retirement community. "When I first started this company, I thought my customers would be like me," says Connie. "Boomers who needed to buy things for their parents or grandparents. But it turns out that about 70 percent of our sales are self-purchases, and about 30 percent are purchased as gifts by younger people."

Where did Connie come up with the name Gold Violin? "I didn't want to use any word that was associated with aging, that would sound negative. Do you know the expression 'the older the violin, the sweeter the music'? That's where I got the inspiration for the name Gold Violin."

Learn to ask *what if…* and you will soon turn into a full blown idea factory.

Media Sponge

As a book developer specializing in the areas of women and business—and women and money—Jennifer likes to describe herself as a media sponge. She spends hours every day reading magazines and newspapers, listening to the radio, flicking through TV channels, and looking for what is new. Much of what she reads, hears, and watches is useless; an absolute waste of time. But once in awhile, she discovers some small gem. Who knows but that a small item in the newspaper might lead to an idea for a book, or to discovering a new writer she can use on a forthcoming project?

In order to get in the habit of developing niche business ideas, plug yourself in and become a media sponge. Sit down some morning with a stack of magazines and newspapers, and a cup of strong coffee. Read the material carefully, and circle anything that catches your eye. It might be a "factoid," statistic, or chart that shows the beginning of a new trend or confirms a suspicion you already had. It might be an entire article—one about someone or something that could lead you to develop a new business idea. It might even be a picture that catches your imagination. And it might be (and often is) an advertisement from a business with a good niche idea. Don't copy the idea *per se*—but think around it: What other ideas might be close? Don't edit, just circle away. Bring scissors to the table and cut up the articles for future reference. We have huge files on a variety of topics; we gather scraps of information for ideas in progress as well as quirky pieces that seem useless, yet stand out for some reason.

What do you do with all of this paper once you've finished cutting? Why not start brainstorming and crafting business ideas that relate to what you've read? Take a look at some recent headlines from *Business Week, The Wall Street Journal,* and *The New York Times.* Try to see if there is a successful niche business here somewhere.

Businessweek

Time-Share the Skies? No longer just the playthings of the very rich, private jets are becoming more and more affordable. How? Just like condos in Mexico, you can buy a time-share, or fractional ownership, in one. Okay, we aren't going into the pricey business of buying private jets and selling ownership shares, and you probably won't either. But what else can you learn from this? Could this be a niche business lesson—one showing *that just about any luxury item can be co-owned in this way?* If you can sell ownership shares in a condo or jet, why not a speed boat? An expensive watch? A Mercedes? Perhaps there is a niche business just waiting to happen that specializes in dividing up the ownership of expensive status objects.

The New York Times

Market Fallout: Year-End Bonuses Are no Longer Routine. A grim article accompanied this headline, one about how high-flying folks on Wall Street were bracing for the fact that they wouldn't get million-dollar bonuses this year. Hey, do you think these folks might be interested in fractional ownership of a Mercedes and gold Rolex? Seriously, this one headline points towards a wealth of opportunities for entrepreneurs. If even the folks on Wall Street are going to have to start pinching pennies, just think of the opportunities that exist for businesses that stress bargain prices.

DAIRY-FREE DELIGHT

Leslie Hammond remembers clearly every one of her birthdays as a young girl. She doesn't have fond memories of gifts and celebrations, but recalls that every year "there would be one cake for my guests, and then just a rice cake for me. I was allergic to everything. I remember the cake from my 13th birthday the best; it was a Baskin & Robbins decorated ice-cream cake. That is what all my friends got to eat; I got the same old rice cake."

Years later, as the mother of three young girls, Leslie discovered her own children had similar allergies to dairy and wheat products. She vowed they would be spared the heartache she felt as a child during birthday parties—both her own and those she attended as a guest.

Leslie began baking and baking... and developed recipes for delicious party cakes that didn't include the ingredients she and her children couldn't eat. She came up with a famous version of carrot cake, a vegan cocoa bundt cake, and dense and gooey ginger cake. So many friends and neighbors complemented her, and so many other mothers of children with food allergies encouraged her, she decided to open a business.

Leslie's new dessert catering business, Fancyfree, opened for business in the summer of 2001, and she already feels overwhelmed by the demand. Does this sound too specialized for words? Make no mistake, Leslie is on to something. According to pediatricians, food allergies among children are on the rise. Fancyfree is leading the way in this niche.

The Wall Street Journal

Hold the Oatmeal! Restaurants Now Court the Breakfast Burger Eater.

According to this article, fast-food restaurants are beginning to serve burgers earlier in the day so you are no longer prevented from having a Whopper before 10:30 A.M., or a Big Mac before McDonald's finishes selling Egg McMuffins. It turns out there is a big part of the population that likes something other than breakfast food for their morning meal. What does this mean to you, the niche business person? Well, it gives you a good look at a shift in eating habits. Perhaps there is something here for gourmet entrepreneurs who have a yen to develop new snack foods. How about a new kind of breakfast treat that appeals to hearty eaters—a bacon-flavored donut? Okay, so not every idea you'll come up with is worth pursuing. In fact, most of them will be absolutely worthless. The point is to get in the habit of sponging up information and sifting through it on a daily basis, looking for scraps and gems you can use. Then one day, without warning, you might uncover your own million-dollar idea.

> GET IN THE HABIT OF "SPONGING" THE MEDIA AND SIFTING THROUGH IT ON A DAILY BASIS LOOKING FOR SCRAPS AND GEMS YOU CAN USE.

Advanced Idea Factory

Once you get in the habit of sponging the media for ideas and information, take it a few steps further. In addition to making newspapers and magazines part of your daily routine, adopt the following more specific strategies.

Start carrying a mini tape recorder in order to make a verbal note to yourself when you drive by an interesting business, hear something during a conversation (or in the one next to yours), or have a creative thought appear out of the blue. Not long ago as she was driving down an ordinary suburban street, Jennifer got an idea for an arts organization she is involved with. Not able to find a scrap of paper and needing to keep as many hands as she could on the steering wheel she phoned a friend and asked her to fill in as a secretary for a quick moment and jot the idea down. "I'll call you when I get home and have you read it back to me!" Jennifer promised her startled friend.

What was the idea? Jennifer thought that in order to raise the profile of the local philharmonic orchestra they should commission a major work on behalf of a famous local resident. And they did: A few weeks after the lightning bolt of inspiration struck, Jennifer successfully commissioned composer Andre Previn to write a new symphonic work honoring the American painter Wayne Thiebaud. She has since purchased a small tape recorder so as not to bother her friends with dictation in the middle of the day.

Another advanced technique is to ask what is needed. Ask yourself, What would make my life easier? Ask your friends, Is there a product or service you wish existed? A decade ago, a Dallas mother wished there were television programs that would hold her toddler's attention. She experimented with a few things before finding one that worked—a large purple dinosaur named Barney.

Will It *Really* Work?

You've read about three different ways to generate ideas for niche businesses: you can update an old one, find one that has worked elsewhere, or refocus a big one towards a specialized market.

You've also learned brainstorming techniques to help you develop your business idea sensors. After the last few exercises you have a long list of potential ideas for niche businesses. And some of them seem like such certain winners that you are ready to put this book down on your nightstand and turn on the computer to begin tapping out your killer business plan. It's good you're excited, but hold on... slow down. First take a look at the next step: deciding whether your business idea is worth pursuing.

Five-Step Screening Process

Starting a business is an involved and detailed procedure. However, here are five fundamental steps for identifying a niche business:

1. Identify the market: who is it, and what it is
2. Identify the unique needs of this market
3. Identify the product or service that serves the market
4. Identify distribution strategy: how that product or service should be located, delivered, and promoted in the market
5. Decide if you can produce and deliver the product or service profitably

Each of these steps needs to be fully explored as you assess your idea for a niche business. Each one also needs to be met before you can be assured that your idea has a reasonable chance of success. You don't want to squander money, time, and resources on a niche business idea that simply won't work.

Keep Your Antennae Up

You've read lots of tips on how to generate business ideas, be on the lookout for ideas elsewhere that you can modify and bring to your area, and comb the media for them. Many serial entrepreneurs (the folks who start business after business after business) admit they are information sponges, devoting hours every day to evaluating ideas. Once you learn to look at the world in this way, to continually evaluate what you're learning and ask, "Is there a niche business here?" your life will never be the same. Keep your antennae up, and the ideas will begin to flow.

Summary for Chapter 3

- ❖ Niche business ideas can be completely new—or old idea updates.

- ❖ Many niche business ideas evolve from ones that have worked successfully somewhere else—in other countries or similar markets.

- ❖ Many niche business ideas refocus a big idea or major product or service towards a specialty market.

- ❖ Niche ideas can come from anywhere—from what you hear, read, and see. Keep your antennae up!

- ❖ A useful way to screen niche ideas is to: identify the market and its unique needs, products and services, distribution strategy, and potential profitability. Do it initially, then come back for more detail if the idea has promise.

- ❖ When looking at markets, ask yourself continually, Is there a niche business there?

Good. Now I have some examples to go on, and a bit of a framework for sorting out which ideas make sense. Just because something looks like a good idea, I should wait just a minute—there might be a better one ready to drop like a ripe apple out of tomorrow's paper. Better keep an electronic recorder and pad of paper with me at all times, just to capture those ideas, wherever they may come from. But an idea isn't an idea unless it has a market that needs to be served and there is a product or service to serve it.

4

Where There's a Trend, There's Probably a Niche

You stop in a Starbucks on the way to work and look through the eyes of a niche business owner. This phenomenon is really something. It started as a niche group of coffee connoisseurs in a niche geography (Seattle) where it is cold, cloudy, and wet all the time and a cup of coffee in hand is about the only thing that keeps the blood circulating. How did it get so big? Quality? Yes, maybe. But there are other, bigger driving forces, such as: more younger people with more spendable money looking for a responsible hangout; tougher drinking laws—and being drunk isn't so cool anymore; small independent business owners looking for a place to meet and work; corporate workers looking for a place to work quietly, meet someone away from the office, or just get a cup of decent coffee; students looking for a place for casual study, one that is cooler and more social than the library; and housewives looking for someplace to get together without the obligation to buy a $35 lunch. So many different little markets come through the doors throughout the day. Sitting at the crossroads of so many favorable trends, Starbucks couldn't miss! Maybe my niche business should try to follow in the wake of a trend—what are some of today's trends, anyway?

Your idea antennae are waving now; we can see them from here! Now that you're in the mood to generate idea after idea for niche businesses, is there a particular direction in which you should point those antennae? Are there hot areas and directions that aspiring entrepreneurs should focus on right now?

As Americans learned so abruptly in the fall of 2001, the world can change in an instant and what seemed true one day can seem insignificant the next. But there are some long-standing and emerging trends that probably won't go away, since they are linked to changes in demographics, lifestyle habits, and the American way of life. This chapter will examine several of those trends. First the focus will be on what's going on (and why), with a trend where it seems headed, and who is already profiting from it. Then you'll be given an idea or two—or a few—for niche businesses that could work to capitalize on this trend.

Trends are everywhere. Some are obvious, others aren't. There's no way to identify them all. The real purpose is to get you to think about trends, and learn how to identify them and the niches they create, and capitalize on them, using the following highlighted examples. To start, let's explore a topic that is on everyone's mind, the ticking clock of time....

Aging Americans

Getting older is a grim and depressing subject, no matter what your age. If you are in the thick of aging you can literally feel it as it happens. If you are in the throes of youth, you can't believe getting old will ever be a problem. When it comes to niche businesses however, the fact that large numbers of people are getting older isn't appalling, but tremendously *appealing*....

Take a look at these facts and figures: Between 1995 and 2025 the portion of the population 55 and over is expected to increase more sharply than any other group. The figures associated with that fact—the dollar figures—are dazzling. Today's 50-plus adults account for more than $2 trillion in income, and own 80 percent of the personal wealth in financial institutions. In fact, they own over 70 percent of *all* financial assets in America—real estate, businesses, you name it.

What does this mean to a niche entrepreneur? It means opportunities abound for creating businesses and services custom-designed for this audience. These folks are well paid and educated, and have a *lot* of cash. The question is, What can *you* sell them?

Reading glasses, for one! Have you noticed how prevalent those little nonprescriptions have become? Everywhere you look, from the grocery store to the upscale department store to the front counter at a bookstore, shoppers are offered a dazzling choice of reading glasses—the humble little tool that most older folks used to blush and hide. It's hard to consider reading glasses per se as an original idea. But now older women who need a closer look at the menu don't just use *any* reading glasses. When they reach into their handbags to pull out leopard-spotted plastic ones, the shame is gone. Consider how suddenly acceptable and omnipresent something as simple (but needed) as reading glasses are, and you can see how aiming a business at that niche would be profitable.

In Chapter 2 you met entrepreneur Connie Hallquist. She developed her business, Gold Violin, to serve a need she spotted—developing good-looking accessories for our aging population. What does she regularly take out ads in *The New York Times* to sell? "The Best Light-Up Pocket Magnifier." The item only retails for $15, so in order to justify running ads week after week she must be doing quite a tidy business.

The aging American market could grow even bigger in the future. Although Connie is currently marketing to folks already in their 60s and beyond, much of corporate America is awaiting the moment when the "pig in the python" passes into that age bracket. Baby boomers, who are now in their 50s, are slowly working their way towards the even bigger numbers. Imagine how the market for Gold Violin will increase in the coming years. Here are a few more facts about the habits of today's 50-plusers:

❖ They account for 80 percent of all luxury travel.
❖ They spend 40 percent more time vacationing in their 50s than in their 40s.

❖ They travel further away from home than any other age group.

What will this mean to the travel industry? It means that if you can find the right niche, and assemble the right client following, you will indeed niche and grow rich. Tour operator Bill Fischer has certainly made this work in his favor—in exchange for a $10,000 membership fee and a $5,000 annual retainer, he provides the clients of Fischer Travel with 24-hour personalized service. Is it any wonder his phone is unlisted?

These same age and financial statistics are what have made Helena Koenig's Grandtravel work so well. What other kinds of opportunities still remain for niche entrepreneurs?

Fitting hand in glove with the aging population are the over-whelming changes in the health market in the last decade. Companies have made fortunes marketing vitamin supplements, as well as exercise and relaxation equipment designed with older bodies in mind. Have you seen a Relax the Back franchise in your neighborhood yet? Who would have imagined that an entire store devoted to relieving back pain could work? But this business aimed at a niche in pain has developed amazing customer motivation and devotion.

Deina Johnson developed her niche company, Seasona, to market products that help menopausal women manage the transition more smoothly. Like the devoted customers of Relax the Back, people who come to Seasona also maintain a close business relationship with a company that can help them deal with some of life's unpleasantries.

Are there still more businesses that can be created to help aging Americans stay healthy and active? Get busy brainstorming in this sector.

Not only does this vast pool of people want to stay healthy, they also want to look good while they age. Products that help maintain a youthful and smooth complexion will never go out of style. Americans are so focused on their appearances that plastic surgeons experienced an extraordinary rise in business just after the 2001 September 11th attacks in New York and Washington, DC. Office procedures like eyelifts, and collagen and Botox injections surged 20–30 percent. A spokesperson for the American Society of Aesthetic Plastic Surgery believes that patients are now saying, "If not now, when?"

No one expects you to become a plastic surgeon, but there are plenty of niche businesses that can cater to this group. Consider an exercise studio that focuses on teaching yoga, Pilates, or strength training to older women. Do 60 year olds really want to bend and stretch in leotards next to 20 year olds? Not often. Or how about a photo studio that specializes in flattering and sexy photos of older women?

If developing a niche business to serve the aging-Americans market strikes you as appealing, there are others in corporate America and business education already entranced by the idea. Much research and experimentation has gone into tapping markets created by aging populations—the surface has only been scratched. You can get on this gravy train by reading periodicals, business journals, and *American Demographics* magazine (a must for niche entrepreneurs). See Figure 4.1.

READING PERIODICALS, BUSINESS JOURNALS, AND *AMERICAN DEMOGRAPHICS* MAGAZINE WILL HELP TO IDENTIFY AND KEEP UP WITH TRENDS.

FIGURE 4.1 Cover of *American Demographics* magazine

Active Kids

Was your childhood anything like the way kids live today? Probably not; ours certainly weren't. Peter remembers riding his bike up and down hills to school, while Jennifer walked block after block and returned home to an afternoon of reading a book or playing in the backyard. Today's kids are ferried in vans from school to tutoring sessions to play dates to gymnastics class to an evening of pizza and games at Chuck E. Cheese's. It's exhausting.

That is, it's exhausting for parents (and kids), but exhilarating for entrepreneurs! Opportunities abound to develop niche businesses that cater to indulgent parents and over-scheduled kids. The same lifestyle trends that gave rise to the omnipresent minivan might provide you with the perfect niche.

Every large area now has a newspaper or monthly magazine devoted to parents and kids. Our neighborhood has two—*Parent's Monthly* and *Sierra Parent*. The far-sighted entrepreneurs who started periodicals like these about a dozen years ago got in early on this growth movement, and have profited nicely by selling advertising to the entrepreneurs who built businesses in this niche. Pick up your local parenting magazine and you will be astonished at the variety of businesses that thrive by helping tired parents. There are folks who will organize your child's birthday party, from the invitations to the cake to the cleanup. Other kids party businesses include renting out large trampolines, blow-up castles and dragons in which to jump for hours on end, and an endless supply of clowns and other popular entertainers.

Another hardy band of niche entrepreneurs will come and paint your child's bedroom in any color desired. "I charge $45 an hour, not including supplies," faux painter Lindsay Arfsten told us. "When I'm not painting someone's dining room to look like a Tuscan hillside,

I'm busy stenciling dolphins and whales or the moon and stars on the ceiling of a child's bedroom. I'm booked months in advance."

According to the Travel Industry Association, more than 32 million business trips in 1999 included children traveling with their working parents. Have you done this with your children? We have toted young babies along to several professional conventions and even a book tour (which really wasn't much fun with a six month old). It is anticipated that growth will continue to occur here, as many parents are reluctant to leave children home during a decade when emotions and fears are running high around the nation. What kinds of niche business opportunities will this movement present?

Hotels themselves cannot always afford to maintain full-time programs on the off chance that a business person will show up with a child in tow; this is a perfect opportunity for a partnership. If you live in an area with an active business travel sector, perhaps you could design a company that entertains and educates young children with day-long or half-day programs while their parents attend meetings. You could do tours of local zoos and museums, hikes, and other outdoor activities. Large hotels might be willing to help market your services to their guests.

Trish Mahoney lives in Lake Tahoe, a resort area well known for family vacations. But even on vacation, mom and dad might want a night out on their own, and Trish is there to watch the kids. She has made arrangements with several hotels in the area who give out her name and number when guests request a babysitter. Unlike ordinary babysitters who charge the going rate, Trish has only one price—$18 an hour, plus gasoline expenses to the hotel. Her slogan says it all: "Worry-free vacation childcare." That is certainly something worth paying extra for. In our travels with young children, we're simply amazed at how difficult it is to find this kind of service. Do you live in a vacation area where you can organize a premium-priced babysitting service? This would be another fine way to profit from the growing trend of families on the move.

Kids and sports have been on the rise for the past 20 years, and there has been an even sharper increase in the number of girls participating. Is this too small a niche to try to build a business around? It isn't for one observant entrepreneur. This smart mom was tired of trying to fix her athletic daughter's hair after baseball games; it was always flattened, sweaty, and "smushed" from being under the helmet. There must be a better way, she thought. There was, after she invented it! What she came up with was a helmet for girls that included a shallow channel down the back, just deep enough for a pony tail to tuck right in. Now, why didn't you think of that? Chances are there is more specialty sports equipment just waiting to be invented....

When today's children aren't traveling with their parents or playing organized sports, they are attending specialized learning camps or other places to polish and perfect their skills. Foreign languages, dance, gymnastics, and even etiquette are taught through organized after-school programs. Do you have a talent, skill, or expertise that you could build a children's camp or program around? Can you see a need for a skill you don't know, but could hire others to teach?

Are all of the opportunities taken in this niche? Far from it! Keep your eyes open in your own neighborhood and observe what happens there. Ask parents about their biggest challenge. Ask kids what they'd really like to do, learn, or see in their neighborhood. Active children and their parents are a profitable niche, so start thinking.

What's for Dinner?

It's not just reading glasses that have sprung up everywhere; what about the roasted chickens suddenly available at every grocery store on the planet? It used to be if you wanted to serve a roasted chicken to your family, you set aside an hour or two in which to accomplish the task in your own oven. But those days are long gone, thanks to a trend the grocery industry calls "Home Meal Replacement," or HMR.

Yes, people do want to eat at home with their families; they just don't want to have to cook anything. HMRs are the answer. Roasted chickens, pregrilled meats, mashed potatoes, salad-in-a-bag, and even those tiny carrots that come washed and peeled are all evidence of this growing trend. One industry report predicts HMRs will be a 170-billion-dollar market by the year 2005.

Are HMRs only of interest to the big grocery store players? Absolutely not; there are many entrepreneurs equally interested in helping Americans bring home the bacon without having to cook it first. Joy Reed, a longtime caterer, opened a small specialty food store called Spoons in an upscale area. Harried commuters and hassled moms returning home in the afternoon can pop in and pick up broiled stuffed lamb chops, delicate crab cakes, a plate of cheese and fruit, or a mixed and dressed green salad. To complete a perfect meal, all you'd have to do is open a bottle of wine (and she'll sell you that, too). How is business? "Booming," she says.

The HMR trend isn't limited to fancy food. The success of Papa Murphy's take-it-home-and-bake-it pizza, as well as several premade lasagna outlets, shows an equally strong market for homey fare. Is the product itself—the food—special? Maybe, maybe not. The niche is created by specialized distribution—*what you need* (a fresh, easy to prepare meal) *when* you need it (at the end of a busy day) and *where* you need it (on the way home from work). Bingo.

There are even folks too tuckered out to be bothered by picking up a prepared meal. What is their solution? They hire a personal chef. In the past, only the rich and famous could afford to have a professional cook come into their home and prepare meals; but no longer. Now modestly-priced personal chefs are more than happy to take over the kitchen duties for ordinary folk. A personal chef does the grocery shopping, comes to the client's house, and prepares a week's worth of meals that can be frozen or stored. A husband and wife, David MacKay and Susan Titcomb, invented this entire lucrative industry, and now have a thriving business training and certifying others. You can learn more about what they do at www.hireachef.com.

Foods for eating on the run also continue to grow in popularity, and many are from niche entrepreneurs. Of course you've heard of the Power Bar, which was invented by Berkeley bicycle racers who perfected their formula on their friends and fellow racers. And you probably know the Cliff Bar, which was also invented by an athlete. Perhaps you can cook up something special in your kitchen that years from now everyone will be munching.

Keeping up with food trends can seem overwhelming, but if this niche interests you, there is a delicious way to do it. You can attend the Gourmet Product Shows put on around the country by George Little Management of New York (www.thegourmetshow.com). Packed with both big industry players and niche entrepreneurs, these shows give you a chance to learn more about this thriving industry. You'll also get to sample specialty foods to your heart's content, so bring an appetite. Check out George Little's Web site for dates, locations, and registration information. There are also Fancy Food Shows in several locations around the country; learn more at www.fancyfoodshows.com. What a delicious niche to occupy!

The Women's Market

"Women hold up half the sky," according to an old Chinese saying. But to many marketeers, they hold up more than half the pocket-books. Although women are certainly not a recently discovered "trend," it is fair to say that there is a strong and emerging trend towards developing businesses and services that are either directed solely towards women, or marketed heavily in their direction. In the same way that Madison Avenue salivates at the idea of how much money senior citizens control, they are salivating equally over women's financial strength and power.

Years ago, women were considered economic weaklings, ones not worth being targeted. Take a look at these recent statistics for a fresh, new perspective on the cash women control:

- ❖ 30 percent of working women earn more than their husbands
- ❖ According to the Spectrum Group, the number of affluent women grew 68 percent from 1996 to 1998, while the number of affluent men rose only 36 percent
- ❖ According to *Ad Age*, women control or influence the purchase of 81 percent of all products and services
- ❖ As a result of women's increased financial power, large companies—including Wyndham Hotels, Tylenol, Home Depot, and even Harley Davidson—are increasingly targeting this market with focused initiatives

If Harley Davidson is trying to target women, the question is, What can you sell to women? Much of what has been discussed in this chapter already falls into this category. The home meal replacement trend, for example, is largely a function of working women. Mom isn't in the kitchen cooking for an hour or two before her family returns home; she is rushing back from the office, hoping to pull into the driveway and pop what she's bought into the oven so it will be piping hot when everyone does show up.

Are women a niche market? That depends on what kind of a business you plan to build. It is better to focus on the lifestages women are in and on those niches themselves. For instance, menopausal women are the niche Deina Johnson is aiming for with her business, Seasona. Her mission statement is "To provide quality products and information for women to help them manage the symptoms associated with premenstrual syndrome, peri-menopause, or menopause," and her company's flagship product, a hormone balancing cream, moves swiftly off the shelves of its online store (www.seasona.com). Deina has based her niche business on the unique medical and cosmetic needs of women at a particular stage of life.

The Oregon-based retailer, Lucy, on the other hand, is targeting women at a different stage. Its stores in the San Francisco and New York areas sell "righteous workout wear for women." Women in general aren't the niche market; active women are. These women are so active they have an opinion as to *which* sports bra is the best one for their sport, rather than just knowing that they need to buy one.

Not all women are exercising enough, it appears. A growing niche, if you will, is that of the "larger woman." Despite the tendency of magazines to showcase thin women wearing tiny clothes, the majority of American women wear a size 12 and larger. Husband and wife entrepreneurs Marvin and Helene Gralnick, the founders of Chico's FAS Inc., have long been aware of the dearth of fashionable clothing for larger women. Their company has quickly grown from just one store in Florida to a publicly-traded enterprise with 250-plus stores around the country, all based on the loose-fitting stylish separates that flatter the over-35 woman. This doesn't mean every woman, mind you, just that particular niche.... Chico's FAS has also developed a profitable niche within a niche; a strong line is their Traveler's Collection of wrinkle-free knits. They are just the thing for the over-35 woman who travels often.

What kinds of goods and services will help streamline the lives of these busy women? Although delivery services Webvan and Kozmo are famous dotcom flameouts (they defined good niche markets, but couldn't serve them *profitably*), busy people are still more than willing to pay extra to have something delivered to their home or office rather than take the time to do it themselves. Women are a prime market for these kinds of businesses. "Concierge companies" that are willing to do everything from pick up your dry cleaning and coordinate an office move to making dinner reservations and requesting your favorite romantic corner table have sprung up all over the country. Is there one in your area yet? And despite the death of Webvan and Kozmo, the pastel delivery trucks of Schwan's have been making the rounds in 48 states since 1952, delivering frozen food and ice cream to a steady customer base. Remember the "home meal replacement" trend? Schwan's has been on top of that one for many years, adding frozen pizza, chicken casseroles, corn dogs, and Southern style biscuits to their traditional ice cream fare. What would women want delivered in your neighborhood?

Women are also being heavily targeted by the financial services industry. Everyone from insurance companies and mortgage brokers to securities companies wants to increase the number of women's accounts. Tremendous growth has occurred in specialized information seminars targeted to women; the online brokerage house Siebert & Company recently held a series of money talks for women in Mercedes Benz dealerships in North Carolina. Siebert &

Company is owned by Muriel Siebert—the first woman to buy her own seat on the New York Stock Exchange in the mid-'60s. She knows women are a lucrative niche market, shouldn't you be thinking about how you can create a niche business that caters to them, too?

SOHO

Soho? Isn't that a neighborhood in New York City? Yes, but it is also a hip term for a growing trend—the extraordinary growth exploding in the small office/home office, or SOHO scene. Recent statistics peg the number of home offices at 45 million nationwide (and growing), and each one of those homebased entrepreneurs might hold the key to your successful niche business. Jennifer has profited from this niche; she successfully pitched a column to the *USA Today* Web site called "On Your Own" in which she chronicled the business life of a homebased entrepreneur. The folks at *USA Today* were aware of this growing phenomenon, and readily agreed. In the years since Jennifer has interviewed hundreds of folks who work from home. What is their number one complaint? Loneliness. It's hard to build a niche business around that one, but the number two complaint—the constant attempts to perfect their workspace—just might bear fruit.

Although homebased businesses or entrepreneurs with home offices might seem self-contained, each one of them has real business needs. We've worked from a homebased office for the past five years and know these needs first hand. Seeking some order to our accumulated chaos, we hired organizing specialist Mary Ann Ziakas to create a workable system for us. She is by no means the only niche entrepreneur who has targeted fellow entrepreneurs as customers; similar businesses have sprung up all over the country to serve this need. In the early days of home offices, many were content to work from a repurposed dining room table or used desk. But tastes have grown more sophisticated as many have graduated to larger, more professional home offices.

In the early '80s the remodeling craze focused on closets and garages, where companies like California Closet would come in and work their magic. Now a similar need exists with home offices— perhaps you will be the one to found a company that franchises the installation of a modular home-office desk and cabinet system?

Once the 45 million SOHO occupants have gotten a handle on the workspace arrangement, what else do they need? They could probably use help with shipping. In the franchise chapter you'll meet a husband and wife team who've built several successful Mail Boxes Etc. stores based on their neighborhood's large concentration of homebased entrepreneurs. These business people could also use help with their bleeping computer equipment. If you work on your own and your computer conks out, you can't just call the tech services department. You *are* your company's tech services department. Keith Posner has built a profitable on-site computer repair business called Heaven Help Us that specializes in working with home-office needs.

With the growing reluctance on the part of some folks to return to the hectic schedule of business travel that was so common before the September 11, 2001 terrorist attacks, a real need exists to develop video conferencing businesses. SOHO entrepreneurs would be the perfect niche to target. And a great niche business, not only for SOHO but also for larger corporate clients, is to install and develop "virtual" meeting capability—video conferencing, teleconferencing, net-conferencing, and the accompanying training—to help these businesses thrive while reducing expensive, time-consuming, and perhaps dangerous business travel.

For three whole chapters you've been encouraged to daydream, brainstorm, and go way, way out on a limb with an idea for a niche business that looks like it might serve a group of people with the money to buy your product or service. Umm… is it really such a good idea, though? How can you ever know for sure? You might spend month after month conducting surveys, doing online research, visiting conventions and trade shows, hiring expensive consultants and market research firms, and endlessly polling your friends. Or you can just read Chapter 6, Six Steps to Evaluating a Niche, and learn how to assess your niche business ideas in a thoughtful and clear-eyed manner.

SUMMARY FOR CHAPTER 4

❖ Big trends spawn niche businesses. Major social and demographic trends are good places to troll for good niche business ideas.

❖ When trend-spotting, look closely to identify special, growing and underserved needs originating from the trend.

It's common sense. Trends mean expanding markets, and expanding markets are more likely to have underserved niches. I'd better start watching the "Lifestyle" section more closely, and maybe read it before the sports page or travel section. I'll check out American Demographics. It's time to talk to and watch people more carefully and often.

5

Taking Your Niche Online

A hh...the Internet! There are all sorts of niche businesses there, right? Perfume, Viagra, European chocolates—all delivered right to the door by pushing a button. Or is the Internet shopper a niche in their own right? Or is the Internet just a fad to be steered away from? It does promise easy entry and relatively low start-up costs for a niche business, but how does one make it work? I'd better take a closer look....

You just read a lengthy chapter on trends. Were any of those big trends related to the Internet? No. It is part of mainstream America now, and no longer the newest and sexiest thing since sliced bread. In fact, all of the buzz around it seems almost quaint. It sounds so... so very '90s. It's like day trading stocks—or bungee jumping. All these are things everyone did obsessively for a short time before moving on.

Think of the billions of dollars that were sunk into online businesses—billions that in most cases never appeared again in the form of profits or returns. What happened? The big mistake was that many smart people suddenly believed the Web was a new business environment like never before, one in which the basic rules of supply and demand, or profit and loss, simply didn't apply. In fact, it turns out that the Internet is simply a new sales and distribution channel for ordinary businesses—a different way to sell stuff. It is a path to execute a sound business strategy, not a strategy in and of itself.

Are there still successful online niche companies to be founded? Sure. There is still gold in the mountains of California, for that matter, but you need to be very skilled (and more than a little lucky) to remove it. The same thing applies to founding a successful business

THE KEY TO FOUNDING A SUCCESSFUL NICHE BUSINESS ONLINE IS TO IDEN-TIFY THE NICHE, DECIDE HOW TO BUILD A BUSINESS AROUND IT, AND ONLY THEN INVESTIGATE THE INTERNET AS A MARKETING AND FULFILLMENT ENGINE. THINK NICHE FIRST, AND WEB SECOND.

on the Web. It is still possible to find niche nuggets if you understand how the Web and e-commerce work and what they are good for. The key is to do exactly what you've learned in previous chapters—identify the niche, decide how to build a business around it, and *only then* investigate the Internet as a marketing and fulfillment engine. Think niche first, and Web second.

Sally Richards, a Silicon Valley consultant who sits on the advisory boards of many start-ups and is the author of *Dotcom Success! Surviving the Fallout and Consolidation,* still believes there are opportunities online. "The Internet isn't going away, it's just becoming more integrated into our lives," says Sally. "The business people already there, even the one person shop, have seen the future and will be ready for the next wave of success."

Business or Brochure?

Think clearly about what you expect your Web site to do for your business. Do you plan to actually make sales on the Internet, or use it simply to inform customers or publicize and drive sales to your physical location? There is a big difference between these approaches. Many Web sites are really just online brochures. Brochures are great sales tools, but not businesses in and of themselves. They are information-packed, and interesting to look at, but you still need to make a sale. And that means having a great product as well as an audience for it and a way to get it to your customer.

A good example of this can be found close to home; in fact it is in our home. For several years Jennifer has operated a site for women called Goals and Jewels (www.goalsandjewels.com) that is meant to inspire and motivate women to be more involved with their finances. Is it an actual business though? When giving motivational talks and radio interviews, she can mention the Web site address and drive traffic there, but what business purpose does the "traffic" coming through her site serve? Is having "traffic" or "eyeballs" ever going to make her money? There is only one actual revenue component to her site: she can make money from the affiliate link to Amazon.com when visitors to goalsandjewels.com click through and buy books. But they do this in very small numbers compared to those who visit her site. Every few months she gets a small check from the folks in Seattle, but it doesn't even pay for the Web hosting fee. One adventure travel site operator with over 100,000 visitors a month told Jennifer he makes just under $100 a month off of his affiliate link to a bookstore. That's not much. Having a Web site is different than having a business.

Jennifer has a niche—she has the only motivational money Web site for women. Other women's money sites are more investment oriented; Goals and Jewels is geared to pump people up about possibilities. It's a niche, but no real business. Why does Jennifer keep it up? Because she wants the information to be available; she doesn't care about making money off the site. To actually make the goalsandjewels.com Web site a business, she would have to create a marketable product or service to sell to that niche market.

Buying on the Web–Niche, Fad, Trend, or Revolution?

As the Web and e-commerce have evolved, it appears that Web buyers themselves have become a niche. The Web isn't the pervasive way to buy—the trend or revolution—that it first appeared to be. So if you're selling something on it, you are appealing to an online-buying niche of that market. This niche is only a fraction of the total people using the Web—many, many more use it as a source of information or entertainment only. What's the upshot? You need to be clear that there is an online market for your product, and that enough people will *buy* online to make your business viable. There must be a compelling reason to buy online (better availability, faster, easier, better service—and less and less, better price). The "poster child" for a large enough market with a sufficient niche of online buyers is Amazon.com; Pets.com and its siblings illustrate a vibrant market, but little online buying interest.

You may find a large niche of Web buyers if you sell a product commonly available elsewhere, but watch out—the numbers can fool you, and if there is a healthy niche, low barriers to entry mean that chances are someone else is already selling there. The jury is still deliberating on Amazon, but they have first-mover advantage, a solid brand, and good technology, and may well succeed. The best niche Web businesses are built around product *and* distribution— selling speciality products that are hard to buy or can't be bought anywhere else. That way, the online-buying niche is likely to be a greater percentage of the total market. Take vinyl records for example. Audiophiles are unlikely to find them anywhere but the Web. The size of the market in one locality is unlikely to support such a business (check out audiophileusa.com). If you try to sell something like this yourself, don't forget to think about *all* competitors— including individuals on eBay. Once you think this all through,

> YOU NEED TO BE CLEAR THAT THERE IS AN ONLINE MARKET FOR YOUR PRODUCT, AND THAT ENOUGH PEOPLE WILL BUY ONLINE TO MAKE YOUR BUSINESS VIABLE.

decide how you will get your message out to the folks who will be interested, set a reasonable success rate, and build your revenue projections from there.

Learning from the Past: A Few Do's and Don'ts

Third generation Web businesses can take advantage of the knowledge gained in the past few years and build better, more profitable niche businesses. Remember those puny affiliate fees Jennifer makes? Just a few short years ago many large businesses believed they would be generating hefty checks through affiliate programs. It didn't happen. By starting to build a niche business online now instead of several years ago in the midst of the rush, you can avoid being a part of the Dotcom Dead Pool that includes biggies like

- ❖ Alladvantage.com. This company quickly built a multilevel marketing business based on "paying people to surf the Web." The money was to come from advertisers.
- ❖ Contentville.com. Backed by big media money, this was an all-inclusive content site that also sold magazines and books. It didn't last a year.
- ❖ Save.com. Visitors to this site were supposed to print out money-saving coupons to use at local stores. Not enough of them did it.
- ❖ Flooz.com. It's unclear what this gift scrip company really did, but Whoopi Goldberg had a nice time promoting them.

These last flameouts were so big that the lessons for aspiring entrepreneurs seem clear. Anyone starting a Web company now knows to heed the following five "don'ts" that linger long after the failure has faded:

1. Don't sell pet food.

2. Don't call your company a cute name like "Boo."

3. Don't spend millions on a big party to launch your site.

4. Don't spend millions on a Super Bowl ad campaign.

5. Don't promise more than you can deliver.

Are there some equally simple "do's" for online success? Yes; here are five.

1. Find a viable niche and develop a product or service to market to it.

2. Decide how having a Web site fits your strategy.

3. Get a URL that makes sense.

4. Make your site easy to navigate.

5. Make sure you have realistic revenue projections.

Sally Richards gnashes her teeth at the sound of some silly Web site names. "You need to get a name that makes sense, and you need to make sure that it is hosted professionally," says Sally. "Don't build a Web site on an AOL extension or a Yahoo! extension; you need to be serious and get a real name and a real site." She recommends Register.com (www.register.com) as the place to buy your business domain name.

Once you commit to developing a Web site, always keep your potential clients' needs in mind. It is easy to get lost in the excitement of flashing and spinning logos and forget that you are trying to sell something to busy people who want to buy your product and then get back to the rest of their lives. They don't want to devote 20 minutes waiting for your fancy logo to load.

Focus on *Needs*

As mentioned in Chapter 4, the women's market is a big and profitable one. With this in mind more than one Internet entrepreneur plunged in to build the premier women's site. And many lost their shirts (blouses). Sure, there are a lot of women online, but what exactly do these women *need*? Jennifer Openshaw knew: clear financial information and advice. "Sometimes women are intimidated by financial advisors," says Jennifer. "But online, no one knows how much or how little you know. Just log on and learn about money and investing at your own pace, without worrying about what someone else thinks." Armed with this belief and financial credentials from her many years in the banking industry, Jennifer founded WFN.com, the Women's Financial Network. Unlike many other Web sites that disappeared, WFN.com has not. It was purchased by a large financial services company that recognized it as a powerful way to market their own services directly to women.

A View from the "Garage"

It's worth digging even deeper into why some businesses have worked on the Web. Back when the rules of good business seemed temporarily suspended—say from 1998 until March of 2000—it seemed almost anyone could start an Internet business and fall into certain success. Business magazines were filled with accounts of college roommates starting up Net businesses with wacky ideas, and successfully getting their straight-laced parents and their parents' golfing partners to fund the company.

One Silicon Valley denizen who spotted the growing Internet business craze early on is Guy Kawasaki, long famed for his years as head "evangelist" for the Apple Macintosh. He founded a company called Garage.com that matched entrepreneurs up with funders, but soon realized he could also make money in the seminar business.

Garage.com started their Bootcamp for Start-ups seminars in 1999, and the early events were packed with starry-eyed Internet entrepreneurs certain that their business plans were on the verge of being funded by the many venture capitalists (VCs) who also participated. But the times have changed, and so has Garage.com. For one thing, they dropped the now-doomed "dotcom" part of their name and morphed into a more serious-sounding business—Garage Technology Ventures Inc.

The Internet craze was a wild time, one you will be reading about in business history books for years to come. Guy, who is now Garage Technology Ventures' CEO, shakes his head at the memory of the craziness. "A few years ago anyone who could boot up Powerpoint thought they could start a company," he says. "You have to be a much more serious entrepreneur now." The company still runs entrepreneurial bootcamps around the country, although the mood of the events has shifted considerably. In past years the panels had names like "Such a Deal!" and "From the Garage to the Penthouse." Now they have titles such as "Surviving the Drought" and "Building a Fundable Team." (You can find out about the company's latest conference at www.garage.com.)

"Overall attendance to our bootcamps is down," Guy says, "but we're committed to empowering entrepreneurs. We still have VCs, entrepreneurs, and industry leaders speaking, but the topics have changed. Two years ago you had a problem with "crowding out"; too many people wanting to get in on a deal. That's not a problem any longer.... Bootcamp is all about raising money in this kind of market, what VCs are looking for, they are much more stringent. Talk of brand and partnership used to work in a meeting with funders; now you can only talk about revenue or field trials."

But Guy doesn't think the high-tech world will shrivel up and go away. He still sees room for entrepreneurs with a solid business plan. Echoing the comments of Sally Richards, he says, "It's not over till it's over. We don't know how this is going to end. This is a big revolution; it's just that the tide is out. But we aren't going back to using Selectric typewriters, we're not going back to driving an hour to buy a book at full retail. The fat lady hasn't sung yet." What does Guy think will work? "Companies with good products filling real needs will do fine." What won't he or anyone else in the VC world touch anymore? "Content and cleverness," he says. Ouch—there go most of the first generation Web businesses....

Guy does have some advice for those of you who still plan to build Internet start-ups. He believes this business climate calls for "tough market tactics" like using interns to do as much as possible (they are grateful for the work experience and work for free!), and keeping your business expenses to a bare minimum by using barter, trades, and even personal frequent flyer miles before actually spending money on things. Maximizing publicity also ranks high on his list, and you'll learn exactly how to do that in Chapter 9. For those of you staying up late at night to polish your business plan, Guy recommends "More Excel, less PowerPoint. Spend more time using Excel spreadsheets to bullet-proof your financials and less time adding bells and whistles to your PowerPoint presentation to VCs."

Let's concentrate now on determining what kind of niche business might still work online.

Online Niche Businesses *That Work*

Make sure you are clear-eyed about whether your idea is a business or a fancy brochure that will help you support a national publicity campaign and sell directly to customers. What if the '70s inventor of the Pet Rock had had access to the Internet? Every time he gave an interview, appeared on *The Tonight Show*, or was mentioned in a magazine article he could have directed folks to his Web site to order a Pet Rock. Instead of cutting deals with gift and toy stores, he could have made even more on his wacky idea if he had also been able to sell it for full retail directly to his fans. That's the way it is for Francine Krause. She is the founder of a company that sells kits for making plaster casts of pregnant tummies, and gets orders on her Web site after every publicity appearance. She doesn't have to worry if her product is stocked in stores, and she doesn't have to deal with distributors; she just takes orders and sells her product to consumers for full retail.

You'll learn more about the power of publicity in Chapter 9. It is an all-important (and largely low-cost) way to drive folks to your site. Another terrific and inexpensive method is to create an e-mail newsletter. This is particularly effective for niche businesses, since you can be sure that anyone who has visited your site and signed up to receive your newsletter is extremely interested in the same things you are. So if you have built a site that specializes in European dark chocolate, imagine the fun you could have writing a short newsletter including not just chocolate tidbits, but also European travel hints and a recipe or two. Jennifer sends an e-mail newsletter called "Women's Wealth and Wisdom" to women who have signed up on the goalsandjewels.com site, and finds that it increases her traffic right away. It is a powerful way to encourage repeat visits by your niche audience.

Balancing a Business on One Wheel

Okay, so you aren't going to start an Internet business that delivers pet food. You've learned that lesson—pet owners have ample ways to purchase what they need, and don't have to go online to get supplies. If you find a niche market that is truly underserved, however, building an Internet-only business could be a smart way to go.

John Drummond is one online entrepreneur who stumbled upon a thriving niche in his own garage. He rode a unicycle in his early teens, but then got his driver's license and "figured out you couldn't pick up a date on a unicycle." John hung on to his unicycle for the next few decades and rediscovered it in the attic, basement, or garage each time his family packed up and moved during his career with IBM. Finally, three years ago, he decided to get back on the unicycle in an effort to lose weight.

"I rode it in the morning before going to work," says John, "and thought to myself, 'This is great, why'd I wait so long?'" But his grand plan to ride every morning was thwarted later that day when he pulled his truck into the garage and drove over the unicycle. All was not lost, though; John's search for a replacement soon resulted in a successful business.

It turns out unicycles weren't that easy to buy, and the ones that were available weren't particularly good. So John and his wife, Amy, launched Unicycle.com two years ago from their Atlanta home. He was still working for IBM in sales and tech support, but within eight short months the e-commerce business was bringing in more than his full-time job. So he quit. "Walking out the door after 23 years was terrifying," he admits. "I'd planned to have an IBM career like my father—work for 30 years and then retire." It turns out John's move wasn't so bad though; the site now brings in sales of more than $700,000 a year, and continues to grow.

Why did John and Amy succeed? Because the needs of unicyclists can't be efficiently served through traditional retail distribution channels. There simply aren't enough riders for a small bicycle store owner to justify stocking more than one model—if they stock unicycles at all. How often is someone going to stroll into such a shop and want to buy a unicycle? But unicyclists really are out there, and they would like to be able to choose from more than one dusty model sitting on a show room floor amidst the mountain bikes. Online, John and Amy can give them model after model to choose from—and different types of tires and seats, too.

Now that John knows the formula to online success he has been surveying the landscape for other opportunities. He'd like to have several similar niche businesses operating at once, but unfortunately hasn't yet stumbled across a niche as tight and profitable as the one-wheeled transportation field.

Okay, so John found a cult product that wasn't often stocked in regular retail channels. What if you have a "product" that squawks loudly, and can be purchased regularly in pet stores? Is it still possible to build an online niche business that takes an available product and gives it a different spin? Edith Woodward did.

Birds Go Online

In 1994, Edith bought a bird. "Just a little bird," she says, "for a pet." But that pet soon got Edith hooked on birds in a big way, and today she runs Birds 'n More (www.birdsnmore.net), her own Web-based international business.

Based in Clarksville, Tennessee, Edith sells exotic birds to individuals as well as pet stores. She specializes in big parrots like macaws, cockatoos, and African greys. As you can imagine, it gets pretty noisy around her house. "I built a nursery on to the house for the baby chicks," says Edith. "It looks just like a nursery for a little baby—with all of the same cupboards and work spaces. Sinks and a refrigerator are important; I spend a lot of my time out there cooking fruits and vegetables for the older birds. And just like children they are picky about what they eat. I notice that they tend to pick out the brighter colored vegetables first. They eat a lot of corn."

Before starting her bird business, Edith, who is 36, was a waitress. She is aware that the process of opening and operating a small business would have been dramatically different had she started it 10 or 20 years ago. "I grew my business along with the Internet," she points out. Her advertising has largely been online—through message boards and chat rooms frequented by lovers of big birds. Her correspondence with her customers is most often through e-mail. And even the biggest boondoogle of small business—taking checks from strangers and setting up a merchant account with a bank—was only a temporary problem.

Once you set up your own Web site, how are you going to take your customers' money? It seemed like a slow process at first to Edith. People had to send her checks, she had to wait for the checks to clear, and then she shipped the birds. As she dealt with more and more customers and money though, she noticed businesses like Paypal (www.paypal.com) cropping up online to help entrepreneurs like her deal with money transactions.

Edith's plan is to grow her business to the next level and become a larger supplier to the pet store chains. Why would a customer buy an exotic bird online from Edith instead of from their local pet store? First, she is a specialist who knows birds, not just a high school student with a weekend job at a pet store who can't answer detailed questions. Second, she has built a reputation online by advertising to visitors of bird discussion groups. She knows where to find bird lovers on the Web, and they know how to find her online bird store.

A Few More Challenges

While the Web provides unique opportunities to define and serve a niche, it also comes with its own set of challenges. You've read about a few, such as sizing the buying niche, and creating a site that works efficiently. Here are a few more things to watch out for.

Outside Investors

Edith and John are in two completely different kinds of Web businesses—exotic birds and unicycles. But they have one big thing in common: they built their companies up from scratch without any outside investors.

In the glory days of Internet businesses, the venture capitalists were revered. These were the deep-pocketed business folks that would invest millions into some MBA's idea for a new portal, or a newer delivery service. Where are they now? Is it still possible for you to start an online business using OPM (other people's money)? The short answer is "no."

Venture capitalists are no longer interested in listening to a pitch for a hot Web business from two guys with a plan drawn on the back of a napkin. Their focus has turned to more technology-driven businesses. Bankers are also more jaded now, and you should be prepared to overcome a lot of resistance from lenders for anything that resembles an old-style Internet business.

What about "angel investors" ? Those were the well-heeled private investors willing to take chances on start-ups and put their own money into the deal. They, too, seemed to play a critical role in the funding of many dotcom businesses. Guy Kawasaki admits that

VENTURE CAPITALISTS ARE NO LONGER INTERESTED IN LISTENING TO A PITCH FOR A HOT WEB BUSINESS FROM TWO GUYS WITH A PLAN DRAWN ON THE BACK OF A NAPKIN.

angels have nearly all taken flight. "There is considerably less interest by angels now. Their personal portfolios have been severely affected by the market drop and they're playing with real money."

The reluctance of both angels and VCs to back most Internet businesses has to do not only with the tremendous failure rate of the first generation of Web sites, but also with the difficulty of getting their money out of deals. These folks don't want their money tied up forever; they want to move on and fund another up and coming company. It takes a "liquidity event" like going public or being bought up by a large company for an institutional investor to be able to get their money out of an investment, and these events are rare these days.

The history of failed dotcom businesses has also had an effect on traditional means of financing. Go to a bank and pitch a new Web-based business, and you may see a lot of head scratching. You will certainly have to do detailed homework on the viability of the business plan.

Touch and Feel

Finding funding for your Web business sounds like a real challenge, but is it the only one? There are some very exciting and exhilarating aspects to doing business online, but there are also some unique challenges only exist online.

Imagine a small business in a retail strip center, one that sells supplies to graphic designers. Business seems fine and sales are steady, until one day they suddenly slump. The owner, who has been standing behind the counter for years talking to his clients, watching them select products, and listening to their needs, is unsure what has happened. So he picks up the phone and calls a few of his old-timers. He quickly learns that the graphic designers are having a hard time due to a local advertising slump. No one is hiring them, so they have a reduced need for supplies. Now that the owner understands the problem, he adjusts his prices downward to help attract sales, and limits his own ordering in an attempt to sit out the slump. He is able to do this because he is close to his customers.

But with an online business, who are you going to call? There is an eerie aspect to relying on folks around the country you've never met, haven't spoken to, and probably never will. The owner of our mythical graphic supply store can observe his customers as they ship and see which products appeal and which gather dust. He is able to gather more information about his customers than a Web site that has only sales data to go on.

Isn't It All about Repeat Business?

Building repeat business online has also turned out to be a bigger challenge than originally believed. Many a PowerPoint presentation before potential funders included optimistic projections regarding how often online customers would return, and how the profits would grow each time due to the reduced cost of "acquiring customers." As more and more Internet retailers began to run out of money, however, the realization slowly dawned that this belief was downright wrong. Michael Barach, the CEO of a well-funded online health product retailer called MotherNature.com, sat down with his calculator to figure out just when his site would begin to make money. What he learned was that the math didn't work. Attracting a customer once was no guarantee they would ever buy again, and the ongoing marketing costs were overwhelming. Barach dissolved the company and returned the money to investors rather than continue down a doomed path. Many industry analysts now believe Internet retailing will only work for specialty niche marketers.

> BUILDING REPEAT BUSINESS ONLINE HAS TURNED OUT TO BE A BIGGER CHAL-
> LENGE THAN ORIGINALLY BELIEVED.

Are you scared yet? That's not the intention, but it's important to have a healthy sense of how difficult it is to build a successful online business. It's difficult, but not impossible. Recent projections from AMI-Partners Inc., a New York consulting firm, show that to be true: by the end of 2002 small companies will have seen their total online sales grow to $120 billion, out-pacing the overall growth of e-commerce revenue.

Don't Give Up

Still, it's not easy. As Sally Richards warns, "There are still people out there who think they can get rich quick with a Web site. They have no idea what it takes to succeed." So drop your dreams of instant riches this instant. But don't drop the idea that you can find a niche, plan well, do your homework, start slowly, get the word out, and find customers online. In Chapter 6, you'll find a framework for doing just that sort of homework.

SUMMARY FOR CHAPTER 5

❖ The Internet, or "Web," isn't a business or a business strategy. But it can be a powerful way to execute a sound strategy and deploy a business.

❖ Identify the niche first—*then* decide how the Web fits and enhances your strategy—*then* build a good site. Many dot-com businesses had this backwards.

❖ Web opportunities exist where a niche can't be served effectively through traditional distribution channels. Unicycles are one example.

❖ The Web provides special challenges in acquiring customers, knowing and keeping up with their needs and keeping them loyal.

❖ It is possible to start a Web-based business. The chances of funding and success are even greater if it can be defined and "sold" as a profitable niche business.

OK, so the Internet isn't the end-all solution. Yet if used just right, it may be a viable tool or tactic to promote and deliver my niche product to my niche. Just the same, I'd better be careful. I need to keep it in perspective, since I know money and customers won't come to me just because my product's on the Web. I've gotta find the right business, then consider whether and how the Web will make it better....

6

Six Steps to
Evaluating a Niche

You step out of the shower and reflexively reach for a towel. Your mind's going a mile a minute (and for once, not in the middle of the night). You think you've got it; a niche business idea sure to knock the socks off that special little market, and be doable and financially viable. It's an EVENING "day" care/kid camp center—for parents looking for a spontaneous night out without the hassle of finding a baby sitter. For parents working late, on their house, or the swing shift, or traveling. For kids bored with the *same old home evening routine. It's the same as the multitude of day care centers, but with different hours of operation. You stand there—dripping wet—and the second-guessing process starts. Is the market big enough? Are there enough customers with reason to buy and buy again to make this thing thrive? How will you reach them? And will some NYSE-traded or franchise giant open a business or offer a similar product right next door? Does the idea hold water, or is it "dripping wet" to begin with? So many questions to answer. The first few are the most important—does that niche market exist? And how big is it? Do you really have a product to deliver it? Before rolling the dice and advancing any further, these questions must be answered—without shooting your "wad" on expensive market research.*

How do you analyze a market once a "golden idea" pops into your head? If you want to do it quickly and at a reasonable price, read on....

Approaches to marketing and market analysis are as numerous as marketers themselves. Marketing in the real world is an "art and science" proposition, where judgment and good sense come together with pieces of data, anecdotes, and experiences to produce a market and business scenario. With the same set of paints and motif in front of them, everybody draws a slightly different picture.

That said, here is one approach that also serves as a roadmap to this chapter.

A Six Step Approach to Sizing a Niche Market

Step 1. *Define your market target.* This means clearly defining the market niche, and its needs and key attributes. Later you'll find a four-step guide to deciding if you have a niche—and if it is a relevant market target for a business.

Step 2. *Define your product or service.* This step would seem out of place as part of a method to size or "check out" a market. But in terms of niche businesses, it is the product that makes the niche relevant. Left-handed Italian-Americans could be considered a niche market, but if you have nothing to market to them, so what? It's particularly important—and useful—to define a *business theme* and position a product—with a *value proposition*—before going any further. Even if it seems like a detour from the literal task of market sizing, in the niche case, it's essential.

Step 3. *Tune in to the market.* Raise your antennae, tune in, listen, and get a feel for the true needs and nature of the market. Market researchers call this "qualitative research"—looking for "directional" interest in an idea, but stopping short of placing specific numbers on the size of a market. There are many informal techniques for pulling this off (and that's good, because formal ones are expensive). Common sense rules.

Step 4. *Gather numbers.* In marketing, a number is a valuable tool. Marketing and business plans are always more convincing if they have some real market data to quantify the size of a market. And with these numbers, you will feel better about the business idea, and it will form the base for a more solid financial "business case." Below you'll find ways to get at some of these numbers—for free or a modest fee.

Step 5. *Determine growth drivers.* What kinds of things would make the niche market *grow*? By definition, a niche market *doesn't have to* grow in order to support a successful business. But it helps. A niche business idea has more chance for success—and it may be a better one to begin with—if it can "catch on" with more products or ones for a bigger audience. Part of the market assessment is to determine how much the business can grow, either naturally in the size of the niche or by "crossover" into other products or niches. This provides an important ingredient to the business plan, but also forces you to think more clearly about the market and niche you've identified. If in the end you decide the niche is no-growth—but is captive and enduring—that's OK, but make that decision consciously.

Step 6. *Start your financials.* This book isn't the place to dwell on financial plans or analysis, but it is important to recognize that market size and acceptance form the "top line" of the profit and loss, or "P&L" projection. You'll see how the market projection plugs into the P&L.

Step 1: Define Your Market Target

Here is where you define—and articulate—your niche market. The outcome is a *target market statement*—usually a single sentence or phrase defining the attributes of that market. "Retired, widowed, or divorced women, age 55 or older, unemployed or earning less than $30,000/year, living in the wealthy northeastern suburbs of Columbus, Ohio," might be a niche market target for a financial

sizing exercise is meaningless unless the other three criteria are met.

4. *Reachable.* When a niche market is definable, meaningful, and large, but there's no way to connect with it or give visibility to your product or service, it remains nonviable. For that matter, can we even *find* one? Even if there were a product to sell to left-handed Italian widows, how would you connect with that community? There is no newspaper or magazine serving their needs. They don't meet on Friday nights, shop in the same places, do similar things, or even talk with each other. You could have the best product in the world, but it would be difficult to connect it with the market.

Again, the key is to think clearly through your niche market—who it is, and whether it's definable, meaningful, sizeable, *and* reachable. The key word is *and*—a target or niche market must be "four for four" to have any chance to succeed. Otherwise, it may be defined too narrowly or be wrong altogether. See Table 6.1 for a sample market target analysis for some of the niches mentioned above.

Step 2: Define Your Product or Service

As already discussed, it might seem out of place to start defining your product at this early stage. You're supposed to be customer, product, focused, right? But in setting up a niche business, where products and services are being matched to markets to meet specialized needs, it's important to build a business theme and start defining the product right away. It doesn't have to be done in owner's-manual detail, but the concept should be there.

Much has been said and written about product definition and management. Product management goes beyond the physical product and into the expansive world of product *positioning*. Positioning

TABLE 6.1 Market Target Analysis for Sample Niches

Four out of four suggests a viable market target for further discovery. "Challenge" indicates it can be done with a little extra effort and creativity.

Market Niche	Definable	Meaningful	Sizeable	Reachable
Recent widows	yes	yes	yes	yes
Left-handed widows	yes	no	no	no
Suburban minorities	yes	challenge	yes	yes
Italian Americans	yes	challenge	yes	yes
Seniors	yes	yes	yes	yes
Seniors–connect with Internet	yes	yes	challenge	yes
Women needing large bras	yes	yes	challenge	challenge
People with food allergies	yes	yes	challenge	yes

examines the comparative attributes of the product versus competitors, and the message, or image, created around the product. Since niche markets aren't rife with competitors, some of this doesn't apply—for example, its not necessary to devote extensive time and resources to branding. But it is important to clearly identify the business theme and product and how it fits into the marketplace. And the most straightforward way to start that process is to create a theme statement and value proposition.

Was That a Pass or a Value Proposition?

A value proposition *defines what the customer will get and what they will give up or pay for it*. The goal of this exercise is to build a business theme and value proposition that can be stated in a *single sentence*.

Such a statement is the core strategic foundation of the niche business. It defines the market and the relevance of the product in that market, then provides the basis for further studying market size and crafting a "reach" strategy.

Southwest Airlines provides a classic example of a clear and successful theme and value proposition. It started as a large niche business and evolved into a solid market player that its competitors strive to emulate; the value proposition had everything to do with that. Southwest saw a market—a large niche—of travelers who wanted low fares for short-hop travel (less than 1,000 miles) and would give up something to get them. Gone were assigned seating, in-flight meals, interline baggage transfers, large comfortable aircraft, and ubiquitous access through travel agents. Customers were asked to give up those things in order to get lower fares. Southwest clearly differentiated itself in the market and found that a huge number of customers were willing to accept that value proposition. So not only did the value proposition define the market, it also served to simplify operations and lower costs, which lead to greater profitability. You don't have to start an airline, but you can use this important lesson to help in your take-off.

Elevate Yourself

Before crafting the text and stepping onto the stage, public speakers are taught to state their theme in a single sentence. This brings focus to the message and provides a tree trunk to attach branches, leaves, and other enriching elements of the talk. The single-sentence theme guides everything else in the presentation.

A business concept or value proposition should also be stated in a single sentence. The successful niche entrepreneur knows how to create what's known as an "elevator speech." Picture yourself in an elevator with a couple of bystanders. You're on the ground floor, and on your way to the ninth floor. Can you explain your business concept and value proposition in the minute or two it takes to get there? Do the bystanders understand and nod their head in agreement? If so, you're on your way to a viable idea. The work isn't done since you don't know if customers will buy or if there are enough of them. But if bystanders can at least understand the concept you're on your way. If you can't explain it that quickly, chances are it isn't clear or right. You need to be able to explain it to customers, suppliers, financial backers, and almost everyone else you come in contact with. Practice describing your business in one or two short sentences during a one-minute elevator ride. (If there are no elevators nearby, try a trip to your mailbox.)

A BUSINESS CONCEPT AND VALUE PROPOSITION SHOULD BE STATED IN A SINGLE SENTENCE.

A Business in One Sentence

Geoffrey Moore, marketing expert, consultant, and author of *Crossing the Chasm, Inside the Tornado* and other books, has a useful fill in the blank framework for creating product and servicing positioning statements central to any business and to niche businesses in particular. See Figure 6.1.

So you think your market is definable, meaningful, sizable, and reachable? Doing a value proposition will get you a step closer to confirming that, and provide the basis to begin research. You'll have

FIGURE 6.1 Framework for Developing Single Sentence Theme and
Positioning Statement

For _____ *(target customers—the niche, and geography
if relevant)*

Who _____ *(further qualify customers and time of need)*

Our product or service is _____ *(state the product)*

That provides _____ *(key features, benefits, and tradeoffs)*

Unlike _____ *(competitors, or products not serving needs
of the niche)*

Our product/service _____ *(serves the niche by
doing what)*

---

something to test, and it will make you feel a lot better about your
idea. Let's try a few:

Example #1. Personal computer buying, connection, and subscription service for senior citizens.

First, check the target:

- ❖ *definable* (seniors who want to get on the Internet and learn
  computing their way)
- ❖ *meaningful* (this need will result in buying specific products
  and services)
- ❖ *sizeable* (a clearcut demographic; the challenge is identifying
  the portion of that group that has the need and interest)
- ❖ *reachable* (find the nearest "Sun City" or local paper aimed at
  seniors, and don't forget about the American Association for
  Retired Persons)

FIGURE 6.2 Positioning Statement

For seniors and pre-PC era 50-somethings in Chicago's near north side

Who want to connect with the Internet but have little to no computing experience, and are willing to pay more for personalized assistance

Our product/service is hardware and software purchase assistance, connectivity, and training at a package price

That provides access to the Internet, basic learning, and shortcuts at a slight price premium

Unlike other retail sellers, which have young threatening tattoo-studded rappers selling only "boxes," who provide no assistance yet assume expertise

Our product/service helps this group reap the rewards of the Internet for their lifestyle in the way they want to learn.

There can be much more detail supporting the above, but in the meantime Figure 6.2 provides you with a positioning statement.

FIGURE 6.3 Positioning Statement for FancyFree

For Davis, California area children

Who have food allergies

Our product/service is a line of premade and do-it-yourself baked goods with delivery

That contain no allergenic ingredients

Unlike store-bought baked goods and mixes

Our product/service helps this group overcome the limitations of their allergies, and makes it easy for other parents and people around them to accommodate their limitations.

Example #2. FancyFree, provider of baked goods for allergy-sensitive children. See Figure 6.3.

This may look easy, but it isn't. Stating these themes clearly and in a single sentence is a challenging, but necessary step towards clarifying your niche business idea. These statements don't define the business entirely—phrases like "at a slight price premium" need to be defined, and are readily answerable if someone asks. Of course you don't have to use this template, but it can serve as a useful tool.

Step 3: Tune In to the Market

You have your idea, you think you've identified the niche, and you have a business theme, position, and value proposition stated in a single sentence. You have something to test, and can describe it in a way that a "lay" outsider can understand. Now it's time to start testing it in the marketplace—and sizing up the market opportunity.

In this section and the next you'll learn ways to size the market and the opportunity. "Tuning In" refers to a qualitative, feel-based approach to assessing a market; the next step "Gather Few Numbers," is more quantitative, or fact based. For many "big-company" market researchers, there is a defined sequence of activities—you get a "directional" read by asking a few people, then embark on more rigorous statistically-significant (and expensive) quantitative research to confirm trends and ideas. *Niche and Grow Rich* suggests a more parallel approach. It may start with "listening in" on the market, then going for numbers, or with a look at demographics, crafting of an idea, and "listening in" to see if it makes sense. The main difference is that, as small entrepreneurs, you probably won't be funding $50,000 primary research studies, but rather pulling pieces from available demographics, third party data, and research sources already available. This data won't be customized to the exact needs of your business and is known as *secondary research*.

Secondary research won't tell you the exact percentage of the senior population in the western Placer County area that wants to be connected to the Internet and is willing to pay for your service. But it may tell you how many seniors *there are,* and you may be able to *infer* how many are already connected. Using other industry reports, you may develop a picture of how many seniors are dissatisfied with their service or intimidated at the prospect of buying a computer. None of this research will answer your questions directly; you can estimate the size of a market, but won't know exactly. So market sizing can be a back-and-forth exercise between examining numbers and listening in to bring more light to them. For most people setting up a niche business, qualitative research and common sense will weigh heavily in the final market-size assessment.

Tune In

Tuning in to your potential market is a creative process that exercises all of your senses and mental faculties. As you test ideas, observe reactions, and explore possibilities, it is exciting, fun, and enlightening. Here are some of the tools and techniques.

❖ *Look around*. This certainly doesn't require a business degree, does it? Some of the best ideas—and examples worth following—are found just by keeping a keen eye open to what is working in everyday life. Starbucks is obvious, but the espresso stand phenomenon that sprung up in some parts of the country was present and available for the careful observer much earlier. It still suggests there is potential to modify the idea with drive-up and drive-through beverage and snack outlets. Watch the customers and their patterns. How many are there, and how often do they come? Talk to the owners and to some of the customers. Get their ideas for how the business might grow or what *else* could work if delivered the same way. Be observant—not intrusive. Computers for seniors? Hang around in a CompUSA or Best Buy, and watch the disgruntled looks on their faces. When the time is right, step in and ask a few questions.

❖ *Ask.* You asked while looking around, but here "ask" is expanded to cover all opportunities. Ask the guy or gal next to you on the airplane or bus; the person at the table next to you at the restaurant; and your friends, neighbors, and relatives. (Warning: Advice from these folks is good but can be biased, depending on your relationship with them. Never open a business on the "yea or nay" of your relatives alone.) Get firsthand accounts of their experiences and needs with computers and the Internet. Go to a venue where your potential target market may hang out. For seniors interested in computers, this may be the golf course restaurant on a weekday. If you are thinking of allergy-free baked goods, its fair game to ask a few bakeries or grocery bakery departments what they think of the idea—and how many people have expressed a wish for such products. If you're trying to find the meaningful product or service to market to the minorities-in-suburbs niche, hang out and ask a few "market targets" what they miss or need in suburban life. You want to see if people have a need and if so, if they'd be interested in your product. The one-sentence theme and positioning statement built earlier makes its debut during this exercise. Whom to ask? Try it on potential customers, other people in similar or different businesses, or practicing professionals (e.g., allergists for food allergy products). Even "plain" folks like your neighbors or seatmates can offer good unbiased perspectives; they may also know of customers or other businesses in your niche. At a dinner with your neighbors? Skip the small talk about weather and traffic, and dig into your idea; it is enlightening and exciting to review it with real people. Most people like to do this—they get a chance to express an opinion, help shape a new idea, and perhaps eventually benefit from a new product or service. Save for the occasional "refreshment" you may buy for your inform-ant, this process is largely free. Don't be nosy and obnoxious, but realize that the sky's the limit.

❖ *Go to the marketplace.* If you're proposing a product for sen-iors, go to where they are. If there are "active senior" resi-dences in your area, head there. Go to club meetings and other organized venues. Offer to give a talk or lead a discus-sion. For allergy products, find out if, when, and where aller-gists get together. Be upfront and honest about what you're trying to find out. Again, most people are willing to help, especially if you're proposing to do something that in turn helps them. You might also do some wandering around in other businesses close to your niche—watch what happens, see how they market merchandise or services, and talk to employees and customers. If your business idea is "b-to-b" (you're selling to other businesses), then go talk to some of these businesses. Remember—if your idea is anywhere close to the mark, they will be interested in talking to you.

❖ *Interview and survey.* You've already ruled out expensive, sta-tistically significant professional surveys. But you can hang out on the streetcorner or other venue and, with permission, do quick surveys or "straw polls." Over time you'll get good data and feedback, and it may become statistically reliable. Be careful of the type and number of questions you ask. It's not good to ask leading or "loaded" questions that presume a response and surveys that are too long are a turnoff. Make sure the answer choices tell you what you want to know. "Have you ever had problems with Microsoft Windows 98?" may lead to a "no" answer—either because the user is skilled (or lucky) or has never *used* it. And don't forget—people consider their time valuable. It is good to offer token compensation, such as a coupon for a cup of coffee, for their time. You can also find a goldmine of information by talking to industry players, including professionals and retail clerks. Want to know about selling computers to seniors? Interview clerks who do it today in small retail or superstore environments.

To realize the full benefit of "listening in," you should allow enough time to test different venues and process the results, both in your mind and on paper. Make sure you see not only clear interest in an idea, but also willingness to buy the product or service you intend to offer. Listen closely: there will be little flakes of gold coming out of the exercise; ones that are easy to miss, but may give valuable information about the niche and business idea. Good listening

GOOD LISTENING OFTEN REVEALS SLIGHT TWISTS OR VARIATIONS ON THE BUSINESS IDEA OR VALUE PROPOSITION YOU PROBABLY DIDN'T THINK ABOUT.

often reveals slight twists or variations on the business idea or value proposition you probably didn't think about. It may even indicate a whole new idea. Informal research is a vital part of this process, so let your curiosity run!

Surf 'n Search

It's always important to talk and listen to real people about your business idea. But the Internet phenomenon yields another huge resource for assessing and sizing your market niche. In a sense, it is another form of "listening in," but in this case it's on the media and e-commerce marketplace for clues about your niche and business. A search using a keyword or two can yield a pile of gems about your market niche, and what makes it tick and what it buys (and has bought from others). You can also learn if there are other players serving the niche, and how successful they are. Be creative with this; here are a few ideas for using online resources to develop your business idea.

❖ *Straight search*. Search engines abound on the Net. Type in a keyword such as "allergies" and you'll get a long list of related sites and services, both public and private. True, you may throw out a lot of "tailings" in search of your nuggets—since Web searches on broad topics can give a large pile of stuff to go through. But the sheer mass—or lack thereof—tells you something about the market and if you dig in the right places you're liable to find value. This value can either be qualitative—descriptions of markets and needs, or quantitative—numbers and trends that will actually help size the market. Popular search engines include Yahoo! (www.yahoo.com), which is easy to use and well organized, Google (www.google.com), and Dogpile (www.dogpile.com).

❖ *Media search.* This variation of the straight search leads you to articles and information published in the media. Most people remember thumbing through the old *Reader's Guide to Periodicals* in the library to do high school research papers. Media search engines do the same thing, except they target media stories and documents located on specialized databases. Northern Light (www.northernlight.com) and LexisNexis (www.lexisnexis.com) offer extensive search capability for media, business, and industry research. LexisNexis, which also has charges for its services, business and legal information related to patents (see Chapter 8). These sites offer some things for free and others for a fee, and you can usually access them in local public libraries. Go to Northern Light and click on "food allergies" and you'll find an article or two giving market size, needs, and trends ("...more and more children are testing positive for food allergies...")—all good building blocks for sizing the market and developing the business plan.

❖ *A walk through the e-store.* Just as you might wander around "bricks and mortar" establishments close to your niche, it's also possible to explore the e-commerce channel. Chances are someone else has something similar to your idea, and you can see what kind of goods are marketed and how. Web sites often offer more specific information than a trip to a physical store, and you can find writeups on businesses or even "white papers" describing their markets, strategies, and offerings. There may be a "press release" section that is easy to get to and filled with information you can leverage for your own business plan. Gazoontite.com has information about allergy sufferers as well as links to other sites with more information. Be advised that some of this information may be "spin" and not wholly objective—but you get the idea.

❖ *News and other portals.* There's no structured way to do this, but it's always a good idea to keep an eye on a few news sources, such as Yahoo! Finance. Why? Suppose you're following the computer industry for the computers-for-seniors idea. Watching for news stories about major computer manufacturers and dealers can lead you to new and useful information. When International Data Group (IDG) or Forrester Research publish their quarterly surveys on computer sales and Internet usage, file this information away for future reference.

While the Internet is an exceptional tool for quickly locating information about almost anything, don't rely on it too much. You can easily get lost or off track. If your niche is a good one and the business idea is on target, you shouldn't have to dig too deeply in the Internet haystack.

Step 4: Gather Numbers

As mentioned earlier, a number is a valuable tool when it comes to marketing. Specific numbers add richness and confidence to a business idea and plan. But remember that specific data customized and

SPECIFIC NUMBERS ADD RICHNESS AND CONFIDENCE TO A BUSINESS IDEA AND PLAN.

tuned to the exact niche you're trying to hit is unlikely to exist; if it does, it may be expensive to acquire. And if it doesn't, creating it through professional research is usually prohibitively expensive.

Still, the world is full of data—all kinds, for all purposes, and from many sources, both public and private. Like qualitative information, numbers are powerful and can be used creativity; however, it takes sound judgment to decide what ones to use and how. Below you'll find information on what data is available and find it—in many cases for free (or reasonably cheap).

Kinds of Data

Information that helps to qualify and quantify markets usually falls into one of four types:

Demographic Data. Measurment of a population by its key descriptive attributes. Standard demographic attributes include age, income, occupation, education level, home ownership, type of neighborhood, and number of children. The complete list is extensive, and the data is collected on the entire U.S. population. U.S. census data—the primary source—is tabulated at all levels, from national to state, city, and "census blocks" consisting of as few as ten households. Demographics are a good place to start in sizing a market. For example, if you want to sell computers to seniors, it is easy to find out how many live in a given area. The largest and original source of demographic data is, of course, the U.S. Census (www.census.gov); many data service providers such as Claritas (www.claritas.com) and DemographicsNow (www.demographic snow.com) also provide repackaged data. See Figure 6.4 for a screenshot of Claritas.com.

FIGURE 6.4 Data Service Provider Claritas

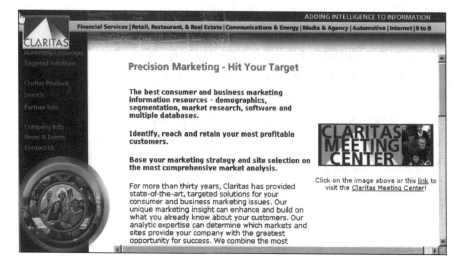

DON'T IGNORE THE PACKAGE

Data can be packaged and presented in different ways.

- *Straight data.* This is simply the number or percent pertaining to an attribute for a group: for example, 35 percent of the people in City XYZ are older than 65. There is a lot of straight data available for free. More detailed or geography-specific data may cost, but usually not much. A Claritas SiteReport for a particular area costs $40–80 depending on what data you're looking for.

- *Trends.* Sometimes it's the trend that's important—the growth of a particular group in a geographic area for instance. Some data sources will clearly identify trends for you; other times you have to compare say 1980, 1990, and 2000 census data to pick up the trend.

- *Crosstabulations or "crosstabs."* These measure one attribute against another: for example, 15 percent of people in City XYZ are older than 65 *and* connected to the Internet. Prepackaged information sources have some crosstabulated data, but there are so many combinations that you'll be lucky if you find the ones you want, especially if they are three, four, and more variables deep. Many data services allow you to construct your own crosstab report; this can cost about $1,000.

- *Maps.* Some may find a map to be worth more than a long list of numbers. Detailed maps can be constructed (usually for a fee) to pinpoint and measure demographic and other attributes.

The more advanced the data package, the more likely it is to be "fee based," but as with most things, you get what you pay for.

Psychographics, Interests, Preferences. Many market researchers might separate these, but psychographics refer to individual tastes, preferences, and tradeoffs (for example, someone might choose to watch TV rather than attend a sporting event in person). Many of these relate directly to buying decisions and behavior. Interests and preferences can be derived from things like magazine subscriptions, surveys, and "warranty cards"; this information is collected by massive data warehouse services and made available to direct marketers and others. It is difficult to get for free, but if you're thinking of a business catering to boaters, it might be useful to buy information on boat interest, in turn reflecting boat ownership or subscription to boating magazines.

Segments and Clusters. Some of the same data service companies that put together packaged demographic, psychographic, and interest information go a step further and put people into identifiable socioeconomic groups for marketeers of all feathers. One of the best and most enlightening set of prepackaged "lifestyle clusters" comes from Claritas Inc. Combining demographics, interests, psychographics, purchase history, and everything else they can find, they

TABLE 6.2 Claritas PRIZM Clusters

Blue Blood Estates	Country Squires	Big City Bend	Single City Blues
Blue Highways	Winner's Circle	God's Country	Old Yankee Rows
Hispanic Mix	Rustic Elders	Executive Suites	Big Fish, Small Pond
Mid-City Mix	Inner Cities	Back Country Folks	Pools & Patios
Greenbelt Families	Latino America	Smalltown Downtown	Scrub Pine Flats
Kids & Cul-de-Sacs	Young Influentials	Middleburg Managers	Hometown Retired
Hard Scrabble	Urban Gold Coast	New Empty Nests	Boomtown Singles
Family Scramble	Money & Brains	Boomers & Babies	Starter Families
Southside City	Young Literati	Suburban Sprawl	Sunset City Blues
Golden Ponds	American Dreams	Blue Chip Blues	Military Quarters
Rural Industria	Bohemian Mix	Upstarts & Seniors	Big Sky Families
Norma Raeville	Second City Elite	New Beginnings	New Eco-topia
Mines & Mills	Upward Bound	Mobility Blues	River City, USA
Agri-business	Gray Power	Urban Achievers	Grain Belt
Shotguns & Pickups			

group people into distinct—and aptly described—clusters. Their "PRIZM" set of 62 cluster definitions is classic. See Table 6.2.

These names are very descriptive and you probably know or have observed people from all of these groups. It's fun to classify yourself and all your friends and past acquaintences; it can also be a powerful marketing tool. You can understand the makeup of your community from this perspective, and visualize how your product or service would "fly" with these different groups. Claritas provides greater depth and description on each of these clusters—what they like, do, and buy. Fee-based services using PRIZM quantify and map clusters by geography. Claritas Express (www.claritasexpress.com) gives snapshots showing the five top clusters in a zip code. In Granite Bay, California, for example, they are

- Blue Blood Estates
- Winner's Circle
- Kids & Cul-de-Sacs
- Country Squires
- Upstarts & Seniors

Digging deeper, you see that Blue Blood Estates is

- Elite, super-rich familes
- Age group 45–64
- Professional
- Household income $135,900
- 1.2 percent of U.S. households in total (paid service will tell you the percentage in Granite Bay)

They are most likely to

- Belong to a healthclub
- Visit Eastern Europe
- Buy classical music

- Watch *Wall Street Week*
- Read *Architectural Digest*

They live in places like
- Scottsdale, Arizona
- Lake Forest, Illinois
- New Canaan, Connecticut

What does this tell you? Well, a drive-thru taco restaurant may not work in this neighborhood, but pick-up-and-delivery dry cleaning, French food catering, or in-home physical training and massage service might. This may not seem like "quantitative analysis" providing specific numbers for the business plan, but it is *based on* it. Digging deeper can actually give numbers on the percent—and trends—of each group in an area. If you're in California you might think it irrelevant that Blue Blood Estates live in Scottsdale, Arizona. However, you can examine Scottsdale in person, on the Internet, by phone book, or throught the chamber of commerce to find out what kinds of things are available and have succeeded in that marketplace.

Research Data. This last category of information comes from research done by private parties, public institutions, universities, and private research companies. You'll find much of this information through Internet category searches, and it goes wide and deep; some is free, some is for fee. If you're trying to find out what portion of the population has allergies, that data is available from the National Center for Health Statistics at the Centers for Disease Control, a government agency. It is sliced into different population groups based on age, sex, income level, and geography, and can be used to size a market. Your search will usually provide a list of

FIGURE 6.5 Claritas Express Main Page

agencies and sources for this kind of research. Private companies, such as Forrester Research, International Data Group, Gartner Group, and A.C. Nielsen, conduct extensive research into certain product fields and industries. It's also a good idea to check the

FIGURE 6.6 Claritas PRIZM Clusters

THE MAGAZINE RACK

The Internet may be the information superhighway, but sometimes it's worth taking to the old two-lane road. You never know what you'll find. Scanning magazines like *Business Week, Forbes*, and *SmartMoney* can yield all kinds of business data and studies. The problem is, it's like a box of chocolates—you never know what you're gonna get—nor when. If you're even thinking about starting a niche business, *American Demographic* is a must. Its business articles are well researched and rely on information from the sophisticated data service providers and market research companies mentioned above. Over time you will most likely learn a lot more about the niche you're targeting, and as mentioned in Chapter 3, these magazines, particularly *American Demographic*, are excellent sources of ideas.

industry or trade association related to your market or niche—if there is one. You can't always benefit from these studies, but it doesn't hurt to look.

Step 5: Determine Growth Drivers–If Any

Depending on the nature of the business, and your own nature as an entrepreneur, this can be an important step. Growth fuels business

---

DON'T ABANDON YOUR NICHE

When growing a niche business, make sure your strategy doesn't leave your original niche behind. Many businesses have made this mistake. The Ford Thunderbird left its sporty, youthful niche behind in favor of big cars, and now–30 years later–they struggle to recapture what they once had with that brand (while the rest of the automotive world lapped them in serving that niche). The beer market is replete with similar failures. Small brands with a story and a niche (Olympia, Stroh's) were crushed while attempting to capture a larger market–leaving their original niches high and dry and thirsty for the latest crop of microbrews. One famous failure was Fox Deluxe, a working-class, blue-collar beer in Chicago. Long successful with that crowd, they hoped to expand to other markets and changed their logo to a more upscale "fox and hound" hunting look. They quickly lost their original working-class market and never did catch on with the horsey set. If your niche is a good one, stick with it, as Corvette did, and develop *new* products or even new *businesses* to meet a growth imperative. Don't abandon the best hill on the battlefield to capture more ground.

---

and particularly profits, as more revenue can be generated on a fixed level of capital and investment. But you can get rich without growth. A stable, locked market, such as a newsstand in front of the commuter train station may well endure for years. It's important to identify what might make the business grow, and *how* it might do it—through product, geographic, or niche expansion and crossover. But if your strategy is "no growth"—and captive markets without growth are preferred by many niche entrepreneurs—that is acceptable as long as it's calculated and deliberate. Open that newsstand, and capture your share of the endless daily flow of commuter traffic—forever.

Step 6: Start Your Financials

When you feel you have a grip on the size of your niche market and the sales potential for your product, the time has arrived to convert numbers to dollars. It starts simple and can evolve to more precise and detailed exercises. Greater precision and scenario-building can help you—and your possible backers. What makes you feel comfortable? What makes *them* feel comfortable?

A complete business plan requires a full financial "P&L" projection, and you'll learn about that later. The output of this market-sizing exercise need not go that far. At this stage, you only need to size the market niche, and the portion of it that is likely to accept your value proposition. The rest of the financial forecast happens in Chapter 10 as part of building the business plan.

GREATER PRECISION AND SCENARIO BUILDING CAN HELP YOU—AND YOUR BACKERS.

The "keep it simple" approach is actually a derivation of sales by percentages. Some of these percentages will be factual data based on hard demographics and other population characteristics, and some will be numbers you "pull out of the air" by synthesizing the qualitative analysis—the listening, surfing, and wandering—you've done. Make your assumptions *and document them* for others—and for your own benefit down the road.

> MAKE YOUR ASSUMPTIONS AND DOCUMENT THEM FOR OTHERS—AND FOR YOUR OWN BENEFIT DOWN THE ROAD.

The more precise approach usually involves more numbers, and will also do things like "Monte Carlo" simulations (sounds scary—or fun—depending on your perspective!), which vary the percentages and figures used for each assumption and create scenarios. What you get are best case, average, and worst-case scenarios for your business. This might be a bit much for someone starting an espresso cart, but if you're setting up a specialized industrial cleaning service, with a lease, equipment purchase, and employees, you might want to go the extra mile.

For a computers-for-seniors business, it might look something like Table 6.3.

Using these definitions, your niche is about 2,600 people and your estimated clientele (the number that would accept your value proposition and become customers) is 780. Does that support your business? It depends—you have to go further to estimate how much revenue and profit you can draw on average per person and per year.

TABLE 6.3 Niche Market Size and Clientele Estimate

For Geography XYZ	Percent	Number	Source
Total population		100,000	U.S. census
Percent age 55–69	21.2%	21,200	Packaged census data–from Claritas SiteReports
Percent 55–69 income over $50,000	35%	7,420	Packaged census data–from Claritas SiteReports
Computer/internet use			
Percent already online	25%	1,855	IDC industry study–from newswire
NICHE SIZE: Percent more wanting to be online	35%	2,597	Estimate, based on national penetration in all age groups
Your market share and clientele	30%	780	Estimate, based on qualitative research

Now you can see the power of simulation. Try changing the definition of your niche to include 70+ and lower income levels, and to expand geography. What happens to the result? Then change the niche size and penetration assumptions and see what happens. If the numbers appear too small, you may not have a viable niche business; stop here or redefine the niche. Once you're comfortable with the niche definition and size, it's time to develop the business idea and plan. But first you should learn a little more about some of the other choices you face. You might want to franchise, seek legal protection for ideas and business knowledge, and know strategies and tactics for promoting a niche businesses. Then in Chapter 10 you'll see how to build out the business plan.

SUMMARY FOR CHAPTER 6

❖ There are six steps to sizing a current and future niche market, starting with identifying a target market and ending with a financial revenue forecast.

❖ Target market statements clearly define the target niche and identify its special needs.

❖ Useful target markets are definable, meaningful, sizable, *and* reachable.

❖ Products and services are identified through a value proposition and positioning statement, which identifies the product or service, who it is for, why it is different, how it meets the market need, and how it compares to alternatives.

❖ Good target market and positioning statements are stated in a single sentence.

❖ Market research for the niche entrepreneur is a combination of unscientific observation and semi-scientific reading of available data.

❖ Data service providers offer extensive packaged market analysis, usually at a reasonable price.

❖ Good financial forecasts have roots in good market assessments—know your assumptions and be prepared to change them.

OK, so let's try this as we crawl slowly home along the free-way in the normal traffic jam. The market is definable (people with decent incomes and young children), meaningful (there is something here for them to buy—occasional spontaneous or planned evening time and peace of mind), sizeable (I can find out the number with kids and using day-care services) and reachable (signs, local newspaper, schools, health clubs). Whoa—almost hit that stopped car in front of me… better pay attention…. And a value proposition? FOR young wage earners with kids and a lot of things to do WHO need an evening off at a moments notice. OUR PRODUCT provides a membership-plus-hourly evening camp where kids can be dropped off with no notice, with really fun things for them to do THAT allows the parents to achieve their goals without planning ahead, affords the kids an opportunity for fun, but may cost a little more than babysitting UNLIKE day care centers and camps only open during the day. OUR PRODUCT will provide a better family living experience for busy parents, and may be possible to deliver by leasing an existing day-care facility in the evening (lower fixed costs and a win-win for the center). Starting to *move faster, should be home in 45 minutes.... Get a few numbers? Live in a suburb of a medium sized city. Population within a 10-mile radius might be 50,000. Probably the largest demographic segment is 35-45, totaling 45 percent or better. Bet those top Claritas clusters are "Boomers & Babies," "Suburban Sprawl," and "Upward Bound"—this really looks like it's worth analyzing. I'll have to check it out and put some numbers together. Beyond that, I can see this will be a dinner table conversation topic at Aunt Velma's house and everywhere else we go for the next few months ....*

Can You Find
a Franchise Niche?

You've read Chapter 6, and your mind is still going a mile a minute working through the possibilities of a niche business idea during yet another hot, soapy shower. Is the niche market identifiable, meaningful, sizable, and reachable? Yeah, probably, although responses from your informal "listening" campaign haven't been as clear as you'd like. A few people you talk to seem to understand the idea. One or two really light up. Others look at you like you just arrived from another planet. Your product or service may work, but it could be expensive to produce. It may not be different *enough from what's currently available, or have legs enough to engender repeat purchase or word-of-mouth enthusiasm. Heck, your idea has never been tried before! Welcome to the entrepreneur's dilemma....*

While your idea may work, the emphasis is on the word *may*. Any time you try something new, there's risk—risk of all kinds. The idea may not be accepted, right, or possible to produce for reasonable cost, quality, or quantity. For example, seniors probably want computers and Internet access, but may not be willing to pay for your "value-added" service. Or it could end up costing more to support them after the sale than you had in mind. When you approach a market—a new one—with an idea, there are all kinds of risks. This isn't all bad, for where there's risk, there's opportunity. If your plan *does* work, you've achieved "first mover" advantage and may have a permanent lock on your niche, high profits, and plenty of crossover opportunities.

For many would-be entrepreneurs, especially those with limited business experience or start-up capital, there is another potential solution: the *franchise*. Franchises allow you to bypass the "start from scratch" scenario and jump in with a business formula that is at least somewhat proven. Franchises do come with a value proposition. While you get a brand, a formula, standards, access to national advertising, and a whole host of other services you'd otherwise have to create or provide yourself, you give up the freedom to identify your own niche and build your product or services to serve it. Like so many things, franchises come with tradeoffs, but can provide excellent opportunities for niche entrepreneurs in the right situation.

This chapter explores the world of franchising and how it might work for the niche entrepreneur. First, it explains franchising and how it works, then it summarizes the advantages and disadvantages of this approach. From there, you'll find tools to help you identify franchise opportunities and ideas for how to "plug them in" to your niche business goals.

What Is a Franchise?

A franchise is a contractual business relationship between you, the *franchisee*—owner and operator of a franchise—and a company, or *franchisor*, who grants the franchise and provides the formula, standards, support services, and sometimes the product itself. The franchisor grants exclusive rights to the franchisee for local distribution of the product or service, and in return receives a payment or royalty. The franchisor also receives a guarantee of conformance to quality standards. Entrepreneur.com defines a franchise as a "commercial relationship in which three factors are present: a licensed trademark, a prescribed marketing plan, and

---

A FRANCHISE IS A CONTRACTUAL BUSINESS RELATIONSHIP BETWEEN YOU, THE FRANCHISEE—OWNER AND OPERATOR OF A FRANCHISE—AND A COMPANY, OR FRANCHISOR, WHO GRANTS THE FRANCHISE AND PROVIDES THE FORMULA, STANDARDS, SUPPORT SERVICES, AND SOMETIMES THE PRODUCT ITSELF.

---

the payment of a franchise fee for the right to participate in the program."

The franchising concept dates back to the Roman occupation of England (and you thought Ray Kroc started it with McDonald's!). Yes, it actually started in 957 when King Edgar of England reportedly started granting franchises to alehouses; the limit was one per village. Each was to conform to common rules and standards. These probably didn't go so far as to dictate the size, colors, and logos on highway signs, but at least the concept was born. It evolved through the ages to alliances between pub owners and brewers, and came across to the United States in the mid-1800s, not as fast-food outlets but as *product franchises* for complex capital goods such as machinery. Car dealerships are good modern consumer-market examples of such franchises today.

The more widely known and popular *business format franchises* became popular in the 1950s, and were driven by economies of standardization, widespread travel, mass media advertising, and a host of other forces. They are a complete package, including a marketing plan and materials, a brand, specific processes and procedures, centralized assistance, procurement, and business development functions. The ubiquitous fast-food and service franchises you see alongside roadways or listed in phone books are business format franchises; this is also the type discussed in this book.

BUSINESS FORMAT FRANCHISES ARE A COMPLETE PACKAGE, INCLUDING A MARKETING PLAN AND MATERIALS, A BRAND, SPECIFIC PROCESSES AND PROCEDURES, CENTRALIZED ASSISTANCE, PROCUREMENT, AND BUSINESS DEVELOPMENT FUNCTIONS.

The Franchise Landscape

There are literally hundreds of franchise opportunities. According to the International Franchise Association (IFA), there are 800 franchisors supporting 320,000 franchised small business outlets in the United States. These range from huge ones (McDonald's and Radio Shack) to tiny upstarts with just a few homebased outlets.

Franchises ring up $1 trillion in sales, which is 40 percent of all retail sales in the United States. Many are single outlets in a defined territory fully owned by one entrepreneur, while others are part of a group in a large territory owned by a single entrepreneur. Then there are those, usually in the fast-food arena, owned and developed by corporations. Franchises cut across a wide swath of business areas. Many of the larger, more famous ones are "b-to-c" (business-to-consumer) operations, but a great many more are "b-to-b" (business-to-business) concerns. As you might expect, fees and royalties—and services provided—are generally higher with the more widely known franchise names.

Figure 7.1 is from the "Franchise Opportunities" section of Entrepreneur.com (www.entrepreneur.com/franchise_zone) and shows the breadth of franchise offerings. There are 14 broad categories of businesses available. Within each category, there are as many as a dozen subcategories. Each subcategory includes one or many franchises. This landscape can be further subdivided into homebased, "top 500," "fastest growing," franchises, and geographic regions and required investment capital.

Franchise Services

Franchises provide a number of key business assets and services, all of which are geared towards making the new business "outlet" as

FIGURE 7.1 Sample Franchise Opportunity Categories

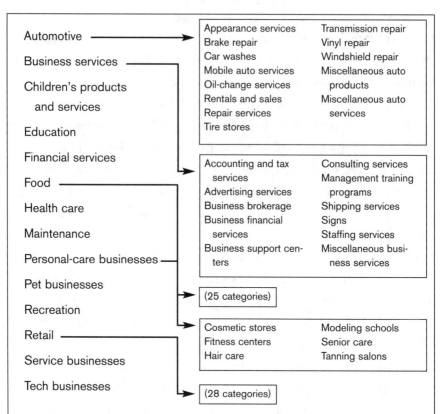

ready to go as possible. These assets and services cover a wide range of business needs, including intellectual property, marketing and market development, and operations development and support. Many of these items would cost a new business owner a great deal of investment and time to replicate. The following are some of the many services provided by franchises:

❖ *Intellectual property.* The fact that the franchisor provides the business idea is obvious. But it goes further; franchisors also provide

- *trademarks*
- *patents*
- *research and development,* and product design and testing

❖ *Marketing development and services.* These include a design, physical collateral, and market knowledge and analysis to aid a franchisee in his/her business:
  - *Brand and brand framework.* This includes name, tag lines, message, signs, and letterheads.
  - *Design framework.* This includes store interior design, logos, colors, special fixtures.
  - *Cooperative advertising.* Franchisors create ad copy and campaigns, franchisees partially fund these activities and get local outlet names mentioned in ads.
  - *National referral network.* Franchisors maintain toll free numbers, Web sites, etc., and customers within a territory are referred to the franchisee.
  - *Territory definition and rights.* Many franchises come with a predefined territory with market research and potential already identified.

❖ *Operational development and services.* Franchisors provide procedures, tools, processes, and training to help a new business get started.
  - *Manuals and procedures.*
  - *Collective purchasing power* and processes. Through the franchisor, the franchisee often gets access to centralized procurement of inventory, business fixtures, and supplies, which provides standardization and often reduces costs.
  - *Quality control.* By purchasing collectively and from approved suppliers, franchisees get more consistent quality.

- *Training.* Franchisees go through (usually) extensive train-ing, and training materials are provided for employees. Employee recruiting and personnel practices are usually provided.
- *Financial services.* Accounting systems (and sometimes software) are provided, and some franchisors help arrange or provide financing.
- *Performance standards.* Franchises usually come with spe-cific operating guidelines and formulas for success—and dealing with failure.
- *Operational research and development.* Many franchises help franchisees by researching new operating procedures designed to improve efficiency. For example, those little alu-minum French-fry scoops at McDonald's were probably pro-vided by this kind of effort in the interest of portion control.

❖ *Other services.* Franchises sometimes help in areas specific to the nature of the business being considered.
- *Real estate services.* Many franchises provide extensive site location analysis based on demographics, traffic patterns, and physical visibility. Some actually manage the con-struction process, and many do location openings and opening campaigns.
- *Community.* By their very nature, franchisors create a com-munity of franchisees that "network" to share business experience, seek advice, and recommend changes.
- *Help desk.* Many franchisors offer free "help desk" services to answer franchisee questions.
- *Consulting.* All types of consulting may be provided, usu-ally for a fee.

    – *Termination and buyout.* There are specific and defined procedures for managing the disposition of a franchise by choice, by death, and so forth. The franchisee often has a clearer exit path through a better-defined secondary market than a regular business might.

This list includes most of the things you need to run *any* successful business. Providing some of these assets and acquiring some of these services can be very costly both financially and time-wise, particularly when starting from scratch. A well-funded independent business with time to invest and create all this may be on equal footing, but most new endeavors—niche or otherwise—start at a disadvantage. Some of the above features, like a "help desk" to answer your questions when something goes wrong, may never be available. The idea that there's someone there committed to helping you through business issues is comforting to many a small business person.

Deina Johnson operated several Merle Norman Cosmetics franchises before starting her own company, Seasona.com. What did she like most about working with Merle Norman? "They give you such good corporate support, and make training employees simplified but detailed enough to make you a professional in a very short time. The marketing tools were good, and they were very helpful when it came to scouting out locations." What ultimately prompted Deina to go off on her own and found a more entrepreneurial effort was the rigid buying policy: "You had to buy all of your supplies like sponges and accessories from them, frequently paying more than if you'd been able to buy them from other sources." Deina does recommend the franchise experience, though, particularly for first-time business people.

Franchise Costs

They sound good, with so many benefits, but you were waiting for the inevitable bad news. Yes—all of these services come at a cost. And it's a fairly substantial one at that, for many franchises.

It can cost a million dollars or more to put a McDonald's on the ground. True, a great portion of this upfront expense is in acquiring the building and real estate. You might spend the same amount to open Harry's Hamburgers at a busy freeway interchange. But there are expenses unique to the franchise that must be evaluated against the benefits.

> THE COST OF OPENING A FRANCHISE CAN BE SUBSTANTIAL—IT CAN COST MORE THAN A MILLION DOLLARS TO PUT A McDONALD'S ON THE GROUND.

The cost of opening a franchise breaks down into three categories: start-up costs, franchise fees, and royalties. As the names imply, the first two are "upfront" costs, while royalties are paid on an ongoing basis.

❖ *Start-up costs* are what you pay to acquire the facility, outfit it, initialize working capital (such as inventory, initial cash, deposits), attend training courses, purchase licenses, get legal advice and hook up utilities. These expenses would be incurred in starting a nonfranchise business, but the nature and requirements of a franchise, such as design guidelines and special fixtures and equipment, might make its start-up costs higher. Start-up costs for some homebased franchises might be as low as $5,000, but could be $1 million for an expensive retail presence in prime locations required by some franchises. Food-service franchises tend to have high start-up costs—often in the $200,000 to $400,000 range—because of in-store food service equipment. Other retail franchises, or service franchises with a retail presence, are somewhat lower; Mail Boxes Etc. estimates start-up costs at $125,000 to $195,000.

❖ *Franchise fees* are the upfront fees charged by the franchisor to grant the franchise. They include the price for the privilege of owning the franchise and using the brand, as well as for training, procedure manuals, and certain other start-up materials. Franchise fees vary widely. Some franchisors charge higher fees but have a lower ongoing royalty; others charge reasonable fees (especially if other start-up costs are high) but take a larger royalty. Fees typically range from $15,000 to $50,000. McDonald's charges $45,000, which seems modest given their vast brand power, but gets a 12.5 percent royalty. Homebased business franchises typically fall in the low end of the range, around $5,000—but again, watch the royalty fee. You can start a "Jani-King" commercial cleaning service franchise for as little as $5,500, but then pay 10 percent in royalties.

❖ *Royalties.* Royalties are fees charged as a percentage of ongoing "take," or gross revenues. Typical payments run 3 to 8 percent, but as you read above, "big name" franchisors such as McDonald's and Mail Boxes Etc. change up to 12.5 percent. For the franchisee, royalty fees are often the most difficult to swallow, especially if they operate in businesses with thin profit margins, such as restaurants and food service.

In addition to the costs of opening and sustaining a franchise, most franchisors have requirements for owner net worth and liquidity. The goal, of course, is to make sure the franchise is well-funded and doesn't run into financial difficulties at the outset. Many of the smaller or homebased franchises require a net worth in the $50,000 to $100,000 range, with liquid net worth (nonretirement cash and securities, usually excluding real estate, and after paying franchise fees) between $10,000 and $50,000. Mail Boxes Etc. requires $150,000 in net worth with $45,000 liquid. McDonald's only requires $100,000 liquid. In general, the more prominent the franchise and the higher the start-up costs and business volume, the higher the net worth and liquidity requirements.

> THE MORE PROMINENT THE FRANCHISE AND THE HIGHER THE START-UP COSTS AND BUSINESS VOLUME, THE HIGHER THE NET WORTH AND LIQUIDITY REQUIREMENTS.

All this information comes from the "Franchise Zone" page on Entrepreneur.com. It is one of the best "search" portals containing information about franchising and individual franchise opportunities. A search function lists franchises according to your criteria and gives "costs" associated with each franchise. But remember, these costs are only the start-up ones—you must click through to "A Closer Look" summary for each franchise to get the fee, royalties, and owner net worth requirements.

Evaluating Franchise Opportunities

Now you're a little more familiar with the basic features, benefits, and costs of the franchise approach. The next step is to explore individual opportunities and figure out if they are a "fit" for your niche business goals and strategies and for you.

Information, Please

Where did the franchise cost figures in the previous section come from? Where can you go to search, select, and evaluate franchise opportunities? Remember, there are 800 different franchise choices spread across 75 different industries in the United States. What are they? Are they in a niche business? How big are they? How many outlets are there? What services do they offer? What does it cost to start? Can you do it from home? You could go crazy searching individual franchisor Web sites, and it would be difficult to know, outside of the obvious ones, what names to look for. Many franchisor sites merely provide an invitation to call for details—and get involved in a sales pitch.

Fortunately, there are Web sites available to help with this task. Business trade associations involved with franchising recognized the difficulties of connecting franchise opportunities with potential entrepreneurs, and developed several good sites. For example, *Entrepreneur* magazine has put special focus on the franchise entrepreneur and created the excellent "Franchise Zone" resource. These sites all serve as portals into the franchise world, with categories, search capabilities, and top-50 lists. They also provide a community forum for franchisees and franchisors to discuss the latest ideas, successes, and failures. Most sites give short summaries of the franchisors and their businesses, major requirements, costs, and number of outlets.

Franchise Sites

Here is a list of franchising sites, or portals, to get you started. Many have links to sites with more specific franchising information (e.g., franchise law) and to the franchisors themselves.

- ❖ *Entrepreneur.com "Franchise Zone" section* (www.entrepreneur.com/franchise_zone) has the best franchise listings and search capability. You can search by business category (see Figure 7.2), and homebased, high growth, geographic location, and other attributes. Rankings are done by size, growth, fastest growing, "top new franchises," "best of the best," and others. There are articles and news releases to keep up with new franchises and the franchising industry. There are also resources to help get a franchise started once the decision is made.

- ❖ *International Franchise Association* (www.franchise.org) is a mainstream non-profit trade association site providing many of the same services as Entrepreneur.com. It groups franchises into about 80 categories and has a similar search capability except that it also allows "initial investment" as a parameter.

- ❖ *Franchising.org* (www.franchising.org) is another portal and resource for gathering information on franchise opportunities. It also acts as a true portal, listing a couple of dozen other franchising sites and containing links to studies and other resources. It posts news releases and is linked to some magazines and online newsletters. The search capability,

FIGURE 7.2 Entrepreneur.com Franchising Zone

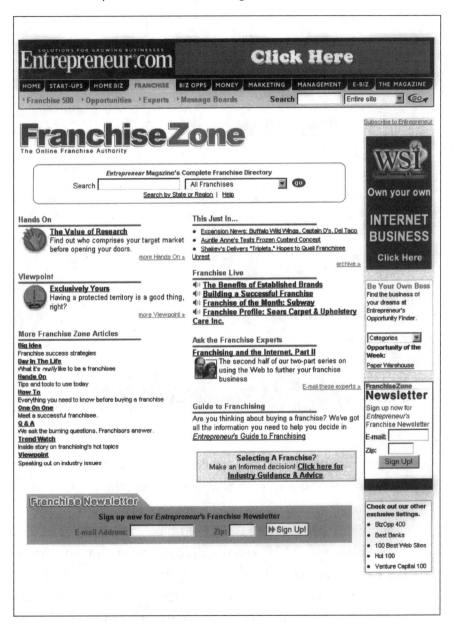

FIGURE 7.2 Entrepreneur.com Franchising Zone, continued

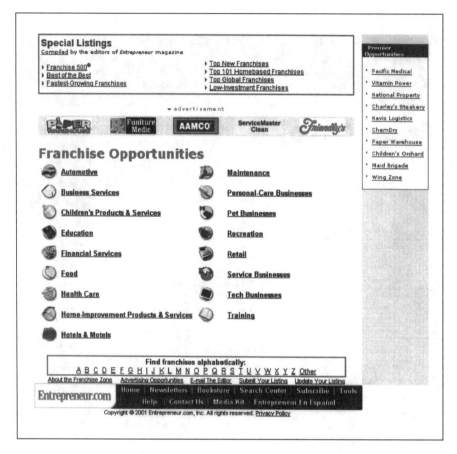

which is alphabetic, is more basic than the others, but the short descriptions of each franchise are useful.

❖ *The American Association of Franchisees and Dealers (AAFD)* (www.aafd.org) is a site that could help in evaluating a franchise business. AAFD is a watchdog organization and active in franchising standards and compliance. It has started an accreditation program, where franchisors who "support the principles of Total Quality Franchising" can earn a "Fair Franchising Seal."

Franchise: Why or Why Not?

Franchises aren't for everyone. Mike Manley looked at several opportunities before deciding to go it alone and open Polar Express, a local ice cream and frozen yogurt shop. It was the frozen yogurt that ultimately made him go it alone. "I wanted to do both ice cream and frozen yogurt, and none of the ice cream franchises would permit that," he says. He was also discouraged by the dual nature of some of the big franchises. "I couldn't just do a Baskin Robbins," says Mike. "I'd have to also take a Subway sandwich shop too."

In the final analysis, you as niche business entrepreneur will have to make a decision about whether a franchise is the right way to go. Once you decide it is, it unleashes a comprehensive and separate analysis of which franchise to choose. That discussion is beyond the scope of this book. You will find help though in figuring whether or not a franchise fits as part of your niche business strategy. First, there's a review and summary of the pros and cons of franchise ownership. Then you'll consider the strategic decision faced by all niche entrepreneurs: Does the franchise model make sense?

Pros and Cons

Some of the key pros and cons of franchises must be self-evident by now, but its worth summarizing them in one place.

Pros
- ❖ Reduced risk
- ❖ Proven business and business formula
- ❖ Established brand
- ❖ Established design
- ❖ Easier to learn an established business
- ❖ Turnkey start-up, less effort—and often less total cost

❖ Standardized products, processes, and systems
❖ Collective buying power
❖ Organized, national marketing
❖ Support and assistance
❖ Franchisee community
❖ Built-in exit strategy—sell the franchise

Cons

❖ Less flexibility, contractual loss of control—you must comply with the franchisor's business model. Harder to stay focused on true customer needs; you are not free to serve whom you want how you want
❖ Limited "crossover" opportunity. Can't expand product offerings or invent new ones
❖ Many franchises focus on larger markets, not niches
❖ Harder to get "first mover" advantage
❖ High royalty fees can offset other cost advantages
❖ Problems are universal—the franchisor's problems are also your problems

To Franchise—or Not to Franchise?

So now comes the big decision. Does it make sense, as a niche entrepreneur, to seek a franchise opportunity? Or should you continue down the path of investing in and starting your own business? The answer is—it depends. (Yes, you probably *hate* that answer.)

Your decision probably depends on three things:

1. How strong is your niche idea, and how committed are you to it?
2. How well do existing franchises fit your niche idea?
3. How comfortable are you with the franchising concept?

Inside-Out, versus Outside-In. Some of you niche entrepreneurs may have strong business ideas, with well-defined and well-sized markets and a great product. Others may be aware of the benefits of niche entrepreneurship, and realize that's the place to be; they may also have good experience and business skills to bring to the table. But perhaps they don't have that home-run idea that's sure to succeed. Still others may have the idea and good business knowledge, but not the start-up capital or time to begin from scratch, and may not be in a position to risk it all on an idea. The first part of this exercise is to figure out which "flock" you belong to.

There are two thought processes involved in deciding if a franchise makes sense based on the above scenarios. The first is an "inside-out" approach, where you as entrepreneur have a strong idea and solid business footing. You search among available franchises to see if any represent—or are close to—your niche business idea. For example, if you wanted to establish a tile and marble repair business, you could start your own, but would also find "Marble Life" and "Marble Renewal" franchises available. "Inside-out" is a shopping approach where you know exactly what you're looking for when you enter the store. If the store has what you want, you consider purchase based on price and alternatives.

The second approach is "outside-in," and it's suited to the entrepreneur who doesn't have a convincing business idea or prefers to avoid the risks and costs of starting from scratch. This approach is also shopping—but for ideas before locking onto the specific product. You're not exactly sure what you want, but you'll know it when you see it. You look through the lists of available franchises, narrowed by certain search criteria (business category, investment required, and geographic location). You may start with certain categories, knowing perhaps that automotive services aren't your "thing" but pet services may be. You find a few franchises that look attractive, and dig further. Of the 800-plus franchises in the United States, many are aimed at mass markets (Pizza Hut, Round Table, Domino's Pizza) but others are target niches within the mass market (Papa Murphy's Take & Bake Pizza, Mom's Bake-at-Home Pizza, Chicago Pizza). And there are hundreds of small niche business franchises aimed at smaller niche markets. Marble and tile repair, home furniture repair, gourmet pet foods, onsite auto repair, and mobile pet grooming are just a few. In the "outside-in" scenario, you apply your business skills and experiences to a proven niche idea.

> THERE ARE TWO THOUGHT PROCESSES INVOLVED IN DECIDING IF A FRANCHISE MAKES SENSE. WITH THE "INSIDE-OUT" APPROACH YOU TAKE YOUR SOLID NICHE IDEA AND SEARCH AVAILABLE FRANCHISES FOR A FIT. WITH THE "OUTSIDE-IN" APPROACH YOU SHOP FOR NICHE IDEAS AMONG EXISTING FRANCHISES.

Kim Wilhoyte ran a design studio and frequently found herself headed out to a Mail Boxes Etc. when she had to ship packages. "It was so much faster to get in and out of one than to go stand in line at the post office," she says. So when her husband David tired of the long commute and hours his Silicon Valley job demanded, Kim had a ready suggestion. "Let's buy a Mail Boxes Etc. franchise." She already knew they targeted small business customers and people in a hurry; it was the very niche market she understood. Kim and David talked to other Mail Boxes Etc. owners and decided that not only was the income there, but a great deal of flexibility would also be possible. "We don't have to be there all the time," says Kim. We can hire employees and train them to run the place." The Wilhoytes are so pleased with their Reno, Nevada-based business they are planning to establish a second franchise in the Lake Tahoe area. "We target the upper middle class demographic," Kim explains.

Kim and David took an "inside-out" approach to their decision. Kim knew and understood both the audience and the need: small business people like herself who were in a rush.

In the "inside-out" scenario, the franchising decision becomes a "make-or-buy" one—if a franchise is available similar to your niche business idea, does it make more sense to buy it as a prepackaged business, or set out to form your own? That's mainly a financial decision, but such things as flexibility, independence, and down-stream growth may also play a role. In the "outside-in" scenario, you should decide for yourself (1) whether the niche is viable and (2) whether you're cut out to operate the business in that niche and (3) whether your financial goals will be met.

Finally, it is important to thoroughly examine whether or not the whole franchise concept works for you. Most niche entrepreneurs thrive on the flexibility and independence they have in starting and expanding niche businesses and capitalizing on "crossover" opportunities. They see customers, and new markets, and envision new products. A franchise would limit their freedom to expand or attach new ideas to a business model. However, the security of a proven business model may be more important—and with so many franchises available today it isn't hard to find a niche business. It's worth talking to a few franchise owners to get their perspective on this issue, as well as their experience with franchising in general.

No niche entrepreneur should start a business without first taking a tour of the franchise landscape. Maybe your idea *has* been done, and the franchise approach will give you vital footing towards getting started. If you don't find your idea, that doesn't mean it won't work; it's just that nobody has taken it to a franchise level. Which leads to one final point: If you choose to start your own business instead of a franchise, you should always look forward to the day when you succeed beyond your wildest dreams and become the one selling franchises to someone else. If your niche is really good, and becomes a trend, and then maybe a lifestyle—the sky's the limit. Certainly McDonald's followed that path starting in 1955, and countless others have since.

Summary for Chapter 7

- ❖ Franchises offer the niche entrepreneur a chance to hit the ground running with proven business ideas and formulas.
- ❖ Franchises have listed trademarks, prescribed marketing and operational plans, and required fees.
- ❖ In the United States, there are over 800 different franchisors and 320,000 franchisees spanning every corner of consumer and business-to-business commerce.
- ❖ Franchisors provide intellectual property, marketing and operational development and services, and offer real estate and consulting.
- ❖ Franchise start-up costs often run in the $200,000 to $400,000 range and require ongoing royalties of 3 to 10 percent of revenues (and possibly higher for "blue chip" franchises).

- ❖ Several organizations and Web sites connect potential franchisees to franchise opportunities, and provide franchise evaluations.

- ❖ Franchise benefits include a turnkey business with reduced risk, proven formulas, collective buying power, national referrals, support resources, and a community of fellow franchisees.

- ❖ Franchise disadvantages include loss of flexibility and control, inability to find franchises in specific niche markets, loss of first mover advantage, and cost.

I get it now.... As part of my investigation, I should look at the franchising world. Maybe someone is franchising "evening care" centers—let's look at the franchise portal sites. If not, maybe somebody franchising day-care centers and camps might have a sufficiently flexible setup so that I can start my evening center using their format and resources. Time to make some phone calls to talk to existing franchisees....

8

How to Protect Your Business Idea

A few weeks later you're in the morning shower again. That evening care niche business idea you had a few weeks ago continues to fly. The niche market is there and the product or service is unique and different. It's never been done before and is rather clever—both in your own view and that of others. You can make the product or perform the service efficiently and effectively. Your market and potential customer "trial balloons" continue to fly. The financial picture, while not yet complete, looks good. You looked at ways to get to market sooner and better through franchising, but there was nothing there. You move inexorably down the path towards building a niche business around this new idea. Suddenly, another question mark appears. Should you try to protect the idea? What if someone else with deeper pockets and greater business experience simply copies and replicates it across the world? You'd be left standing with a good idea—and perhaps little else. Better towel off and start thinking, Is there any intellectual property here? Is it an idea that needs to—and can—be protected?

As you'll soon see in this chapter, it may be wise and worthwhile to seek intellectual property protection; then again it may not. "Intellectual property" has nothing to do with your classical music CD collection, but refers to legal devices you've probably heard of but may not understand: patents, trademarks, copyright, and trade secret protection. Here you'll learn the basics of intellectual property protection and how it might apply to you and your new niche business idea.

First, however, be advised that this isn't legal advice, and every situation is different. While it helps to know the basics of intellectual property protection, that only gives you the ability to effectively talk and work with intellectual property professionals—usually attorneys. Intellectual property law is complex and the processes are very structured. It is easy to go down the wrong path and either spend hundreds to protect something that didn't need protecting, or not protect anything at all. As you start a niche business built on

> AS YOU START A NICHE BUSINESS BUILT ON A NEW IDEA, PRODUCT, OR PROCESS, IT IS IMPORTANT TO THINK ABOUT PROTECTING THE IDEA AND TO GET THE PROCESS STARTED.

a new idea, product, or process, it is important to *begin* thinking about protecting the idea and get the process started.

Is Intellectual Property Protection for You?

You don't *have* to protect your ideas; and for many businesses, there's no unique idea to protect. An espresso stand is hardly a new idea, but nobody's opened one at the corner of Busy Street and Overtraveled Way. You open your stand and live happily ever after on your little geographic niche. Since you can't patent a street-corner, there's nothing to protect—you serve your customers and go on your merry way. But if you have something going that is a new idea, not just a new place, think again.

A Business Idea on Ice

Suppose you invent a completely new kind of Christmas light set. Instead of clinging in a dull straight line to the edge of your roofline, it sends down little offshoots that look like icicles. It also provides extra light and a soft, warm glow to the home on a cold winter night. You design the wiring, production process, hanging system, and nifty new packaging and branding for the product. You take it to a trade show—and it blows the socks off of everyone, including a few competitors. One of them snaps a few pictures, and others lift a few samples from the display. And lo and behold, come the following Christmas, and there they are—perfect knockoffs of your product now grabbing a lion's share of a half *billion* dollar market. This is the experience of family team Dianne Syme and Juanita Donica of Newcastle, Indiana, who developed "Light Cicles" back in 1996—and had their idea copied all the way to the bank.

Did Dianne and Juanita think about patents as they wound light strands together to decorate their store windows? What about as they prepared for the trade show? Did they consider a trademark for the "Light Cicles" name? In fact they *did* think about these things, and *did* secure a patent and trademarks. But the patent was only for a component of the manufacturing process, and the trademark only for that name. Guess what? Other companies easily worked around both of these restrictions and marketed their own nearly identical products with different manufacturing processes and packages. Could Diane and Juanita have had a lock on a half-billion dollar market? Probably not, but they could have had a larger piece of it and a royalty stream if they had made the right moves. At least they got first mover advantage and capitalized on early sales of the product, and a settlement from a Taiwanese manufacturer who sailed too close to the trademark. But remember if you have something special, protect it, and protect it well.

Why Be Concerned?

The above example should be clear: If you have a unique idea, one that seems bound to catch on, it makes sense to protect it. First, it could be the beginning of your own empire or franchise. Take it seriously. Second, other entrepreneurs—many with deeper pockets—are waiting in the wings looking for ideas, and if they find the one they like and it just happens to be yours, that means nothing. They can—and will—overwhelm you. Third, at some point you will probably need financing. Financial backers are likely to be warmer towards your idea if it's unique and patentable. Finally—and this involves elements of the first three—you may *wish* you had been more concerned and proactive at some later date, but "later dates" are often *too* late.

How Can You Protect Your Idea?

There are four ways you can legally protect intellectual property. The first is a *patent*. It offers full legal protection of an *invention*—a process, product, service, or design meeting certain criteria of usefulness and originality. The second is a *trademark*. It is a set of words and/or symbols representing a product or service to distinguish it in the marketplace. Third, *copyrights* protect the way an idea is *expressed*. Finally, you can protect *"trade secrets,"* or key business ideas and knowledge, where there is a clear effort to keep them secret. The latter is a less rigid, but more affordable and sometimes more practical form of protection (explained later in this chapter), particularly for *ideas*.

Patents and trademarks are issued by the government through the U.S. Patent and Trademark Office or PTO (www.uspto.gov). Copyrights are handled through the U.S Copyright Office, and for published material, are usually applied for by the publisher. You can file for and get a patent or trademark all by yourself. But the subtleties and nuances of the process and potential results make it wise to get legal help if what you have is worth protecting.

How Much Will It Cost?

Before going into further detail on the types of legal protection, it is important that you understand the costs. This will help you decide whether the benefits are worth paying for. The cost may be a few hundred dollars or the same as the price of a new car, but even this amount may pale in comparison to what you might lose without the protection.

The total cost depends on what kind of protection (patent or trademark) and the complexity of the product or process you're trying to protect. There are government *application* fees and *maintenance* fees required to uphold your patent or trademark after issuance. You may also require various *professional services* when creating and maintaining the patent application, and these could involve legal, search, and professional drawing fees. For trade secret protection, there is no registration process and hence no outright cost, but retaining professional services for advice on how to protect trade secrets is considered advisable.

❖ *Application fees* must be paid at filing. "Small entities" (defined by the PTO as "independent inventors, small business concerns, and nonprofits") get a 50 percent price break, resulting in initial application fees of $370 for utility patents and $165 for design-only patents (protecting outward design only, not function). It costs $370 to apply for a trademark, and there are a host of other fees for supplemental filings, extensions, contesting a patent, certificates, and so forth (refer to www.uspto.gov).

❖ *Maintenance fees.* Utility patents require additional fees at preset intervals: at three years, the fee for small entities is $440; at 7½ years, $1,010 is due; and at 11½ years, $1,550 is due. This "backloading" helps the entrepreneur and ensures that funds are only collected for truly viable ideas. Trademarks must be renewed every ten years, incurring a fee of $400.

❖ *Professional fees.* According to the Intellectual Property Law Association (which surveys its members every two years), fees will vary from under $1,000 to over $10,000 for a complex, high-tech patent. Typical design patents run $500 to $1,000, and typical "straightforward" utility patents range from $3,000 to $5,000, with more complex entries going higher. A straight patent or trademark search might cost $175 to $250 (and you can do some of it yourself). Add $500 to $1,000 to that if you need a professional opinion with that search, and $200 or so for professional drawings if needed.

Bottom line: A design patent will cost $1,000 to $3,000, and a "utility" patent anywhere from $4,000 to $12,000 and higher, plus maintenance fees. Trademark costs are similar to design patent costs. Is it worth it? You be the judge.

Kinds of Protection

As mentioned above, there are four main classes of intellectual property protection: patents, trademarks, copyrights, and "trade secret." The first three are rigorous, formal legal forms of protection, with a specific registration process and body of law to enforce them. The fourth is established by your own business practice, and provides protection against *theft* of ideas, but not discovery by fair, independent means. Trade secret protection can go a long way towards protecting your business ideas with relatively small effort, but is not absolute.

> PATENT, TRADEMARK, AND COPYRIGHT ARE MORE RIGOROUS AND FORMAL LEGAL MEANS OF PROTECTION, WHILE TRADE SECRET PROTECTION IS ESTABLISHED BY BUSINESS PRACTICE.

A patent protects an invention, whether it's a product, process, service, design, or formula. A trademark is a system of words and/or logos that represent a product or service in commerce. A copyright protects the way an idea is expressed or how it looks, usually in written form but also in artistic design, software, sound, or other forms of tangible expression. The niche entrepreneur is concerned mainly with patents and trademarks. Patents protect ideas—including business, product, or service, while trademarks protect the way those ideas are brought to the marketplace. Now, let's take a closer look.

Patents

This section provides an overview of patents and the patent process. Remember, it is designed to create familiarity, not expertise. If you think a patent is right for you, you should research further. There are books on the subject, and Web sites that can help you become more familiar. Once again, Entrepreneur.com (www.entrepreneur.com) offers a wealth of information on patents and the patent process (and also trademarks and copyrights). For a more comprehensive view, go "to the horse's mouth"—the U.S. Patent and Trademark Office at www.uspto.gov.

Types of Patents

There are three recognized types of patents, two of which bear consideration by most niche entrepreneurs. *Utility* patents cover the form and substance of an invention. As you'll soon see, some things are considered inventions, and some aren't. *Design* patents cover the exterior appearance of a product or object only—not the internal workings or the process to produce it. And finally, *plant* patents cover not manufacturing plants, but living, growing, generally green plants, where an inventor may create new and distinct varieties or hybrids. The latter is probably of little interest unless you have a business producing and selling new varieties of daylilies.

Utility Patents. The utility patent protects the form, function, or method of an invention. It is detailed and intricate, and provides a high degree of protection. A utility patent application contains technical detail on the specifications and use of the invention, and must pass a series of tests to be considered valid. It is easier to qualify a specific, physical product for a patent than it is to qualify a business idea.

What Makes an Idea Patentable, and What You Need to Show

To patent something you must demonstrate that it is useful, new, and not obvious. The invention must pass four tests.

1. *"Statutory-class" test.* The invention must be interpreted and classified as a process, physical machine, manufacture, or composition or a "new use" of any of the above. It must be tangible, describable, understandable, and man-made. To explain further:
   - A *process* can be thought of as a method, recipe, formula, or series of steps to perform a task. It has a beginning, a series of steps, and an end, and is more than an idea. A business idea by itself may not make it, and something simple like coupons, instore discounts, expanding product lines, or new promotion campaigns generally don't qualify either. But a new way of doing a business transaction, distributing information, collecting payment, or delivering a product or service might. The advent of e-commerce

forced some re-thinking on what makes a patentable business process, and such new concepts as Priceline customer-to-business bidding were deemed patentable. You'll find more about business concept patents in a minute.

- A *machine* is fairly straighforward—it is something that doesn't already exist in nature but is a man-made object or tool that performs a task. A machine may have moving parts or be a simple tool—but must pass the next three tests.

- A *manufacture* means it is man-made, not intrinsically from nature, although it certainly can use natural materials. You can't patent a 4-by-12 Douglas Fir beam, but a special beam made of laminated 2-by-4's would pass the test.

- *Composition* is again straightforward—it is a mixture or formula for creating a substance. A new plastic or special coffee blend may quality as a patentable composition.

- *New uses* and *useful improvements* are a bit more abstract, but encompass changes (subject again to the remaining three tests) in an existing object. It's too late to patent a laser, but the use of one to do a new kind of art light show might be patentable. One caution: It may be necessary to license the use of the original product—in this case, the laser—before obtaining the patent.

2. *Utility test.* To be patentable, the idea or invention must be considered useful. If it has no economic value or reason for interest, it doesn't qualify. This requirement is usually easy to satisfy, albeit occasionally with some "far-out" ideas.

3. *Novelty test.* This is more critical: Is the idea *really* new and unknown to the public? Or has it been done before, somewhere, somehow? This is a tough test for business concepts

since it must be clear that they haven't been tried and patented, produced, or published elsewhere. Making belly casts for pregnant women may appear to be a new idea, but it's probably been done before and the inventor/entrepreneur should try to demonstrate a new method or process for doing it.

4. *Unobviousness test.* This awkwardly-worded requirement holds that an idea must not be obvious; that is it must not have been a natural follow-on easily derived by a person "having normal skill in the art to which the invention pertains." Making something in a different color or size will generally not pass the "unobviousness" test. Nor would an easily thought of screwdriver and screw system with a slightly different shape. The advent of the Phillips head screw was considered unobvious and patentable, but variations changing the cross into an asterisk pattern probably aren't. This test, by its nature, is quite subjective, and it is one of the places where an intellectual property attorney can help.

Applying for a Patent

It's important to understand the "what, when, and how" aspects of applying for a patent. Close attention to these details will make the difference between a successful application and one that gets no result or one different than intended.

There are five parts to a patent application:

1. Names of inventors
2. A drawing
3. A description
4. A set of claims
5. A check

Inventors. This might seem straightforward, but only those directly involved in the invention may become part of the patent. Financial backing isn't good enough. Further note that the names are those of individuals, not the business.

Drawing and Description. Detail and complete information are important here, and "the art" must be done in a way that enables others to understand the invention. It does not, however, have to be a complete technical manual. While completed patents are a matter of public record, applications and provisional patents are not, so there is no worry about others swiping your inventions from public records while the patent is in process. A patent must also be forthright about all features of the invention; leaving a few out to keep certain features secret may invalidate the patent.

Claims. This section of the patent application is critical. This is where you (and your attorney) list what is *new* about the invention, and how it meets the utility, novelty and unobviousness requirements. It's important to make claims specific enough to be protectable, but not so specific that someone else can make a slight but meaningful adjustment and take your idea. The "Light Cicles" folks probably made some mistakes in this area by not claiming enough about the design of their product and claiming something too specific about the manufacturing tool that was easily bypassed. If you're designing a new type of drink cooler, don't just patent the specific material or manufacturing process behind one component. Instead, you should focus on the whole; how the pieces integrate to provide something unique. Similarly, if you're patenting the Priceline "c-to-b" process, don't just patent the look and feel of the Web site.

IT IS IMPORTANT TO MAKE CLAIMS SPECIFIC ENOUGH TO BE PROTECTABLE, BUT NOT SO SPECIFIC THAT SOMEONE ELSE CAN MAKE A SLIGHT BUT MEANINGFUL ADJUSTMENT AND THEREBY TAKE YOUR IDEA.

Check. This is no surprise. A certified check for the application fee (see the "costs" section above) must accompany the application.

Patent Search

Before applying for a patent, it's wise to do a search. A patent attorney can help, as can a specialized "patent searchers." There are "Patent and Trademark Depositories" in certain libraries. It also doesn't hurt to talk to experts or people with experience in the field to evaluate the novelty of your product (be careful about how much detail you disclose). And again, the PTO Web site is a good resource. If you see a product marked "patent pending," that means an application has already been filed and so it's likely that by the time your patent application is considered, the idea will already be taken. So view this as a deep-yellow flag. A mark on a product with a patent number means that a patent has already been received.

When to Submit the Application

A patent application must be filed within one year of the first public disclosure, public use, sale, or promotion for sale of the invention. If this isn't done, the opportunity to get a patent is lost forever. Imagine the difficulties if people were allowed to patent original ideas ten years down the road, after others had already adapted and built businesses around those concepts. To clarify some of the above terms, public disclosure includes distributed printed materials explaining the invention, exhibitions, market testing, and sample handouts. The only exception is product tests, where the inventor is fine-tuning the design (not just testing market acceptance). Again, an intellectual property expert should be consulted.

Provisional Patents

A provisional patent is like a legal placeholder for a full patent application to come. It's an inexpensive way ($75 plus legal fees) to start the process and get some protection without providing all information about a new product or service. The provisional patent application usually contains only the description and drawing, not the full list of claims. Once it is submitted, you are entitled to use the phrase "patent pending" for one year when you go to market with your product. A provisional patent can be modified, amended, or combined with other provisional patent applications. So if your product or service is still a "work in progress," you can get some protection, go to market, test your product, and then follow with the full and final specs in your final patent application. A provisional application is always accepted without examination for merit. But don't assume that just because you have a provisional patent, a permanent patent will be granted. And most of all, don't forget that the one-year rule still applies: The formal patent application must be filed within one year of "going public" with your product or service.

How Long Does a Utility Patent Last?

This question once had a simple answer: 17 years. But the advent of the North American Free Trade Agreement (NAFTA) and the General Agreement on Tariffs and Trade (GATT) in the early 1990s caused a fair amount of rethinking of intellectual property law. Out of that came a change in term to 20 years for patents issued after June 8, 1995. Patents prior to June 8, 1992 remain 17 years, and patents filed in between those dates can choose either period.

About Patenting Business Ideas

It's been clear throughout the history of patent law that natural phenomena and laws of nature aren't patentable. You can discover electricity, but you can't patent it. In addition, for many years, patent law held that abstract, intangible ideas weren't patentable. Mathematical algorithms, for instance, weren't acceptable. While this may have displeased the math whizzes in society, it wasn't a big deal until similar logic made it difficult to patent computer software. True, software code is copyrightable, but the underlying processes, algorithms, and methods were difficult to patent. That's been changing, and along with it there's been some rethinking about the patent worthiness of business ideas.

Simple business methods, such as lowering price or stocking certain merchandise mixes to stimulate sales still aren't patentable (they are hardly original). Selling cosmetics to redheads probably isn't either. There is some commercial novelty, but nothing new about the product or process that is worth patenting, and some might argue that it's obvious. But if there's a truly new way, one that perhaps invokes technology or special technology-based processes, to bring a product or information to market, that may be patentable. The recent e-commerce boom spawned hundreds of business idea and method patents, including Priceline. Most recently, the PTO is revisiting the rules and applying more narrow interpretation of exactly what kinds of business ideas are patentable. Again, especially in this new and evolving area, a patent attorney should be consulted.

Design Patents. As mentioned earlier, a design patent covers only the *appearance* of something, not the underlying concept, function, or method. It protects a look, such as a visual furniture or clothing design, but not the product itself or the material or production process. Design patents last only 14 years, but are easier and less expensive to get. The cost to apply for one is about half that of a utility patent. There are no maintenance fees, and legal costs are almost certain to be less. Remember: Design patents are still about the product itself, not the trademark, which is a representation of the product in the marketplace.

Trademarks

Trademarks are words, phrases, symbols, or any combination of these used with a good or service to indicate its source and represent it in the marketplace. The word or symbols should transcend a basic description of the product. For example, the use of "Apple" to represent a computer is trademark-worthy, but to sell apples or other fruit products it is not. Every marketer has rights to descriptive terms. The term "symbol" may go so far as to include shape and/or packaging; the shape of a Coke bottle is a trademark. Trademarks must be physically present on products, but for a service, it's okay to include it in advertising and promotional materials only. Trademarks must be "distinctive" in some way, such as a new word, spelling, or artistic design.

Special Trademark Features

A trademark may seem to be just a form of a patent, perhaps loosely related to design patents. This is not so. There are several distinctive features of trademarks.

❖ Trademarks need not be registered. If you're the first to use a mark on a product, that in itself qualifies it as a trademark. The protection process isn't that clear and may be up to individual courts in common law to enforce. You can use a "TM" symbol immediately upon going to market with your trademark.

❖ It's still a good idea however, to register a trademark. Federal registration upholds protection in all 50 states, even if you aren't using it in all states. State registration upholds trademarks in the state registered. And registration makes it easier to get international recognition and protection, if that comes into play. A "registered trademark" gets the "r inside a circle" symbol or ®.

❖ Trademarks are "owned" as long as the owner keeps using it. They must be renewed every ten years (at a minor cost). For registered trademarks, it is usually necessary to show they are in use. A trademark for a pending business or product may be registered by filing an "intent to use" application. Actual use must start within six months of filing (unless good cause is shown for extension). Filing an "intent to use" application will give an owner preference over another owner actually using the trademark subsequent to the first owner's filing.

❖ Trademark applications are also submitted to the PTO. The process isn't as intricate as with patents, but it doesn't hurt to discuss it with an intellectual property expert as part of your overall protection strategy consultation.

Trade Secrets

Trade secrets are the last—and often most practical—solution for intellectual property and protection. They might be defined as knowledge (almost any kind of knowledge, either business or technical) that is kept secret for the purpose of gaining business advantage over competitors. Any form of knowledge is protectable, whether it's a business idea, a product idea, a formula, a process, customer information and research, a supplier agreement, cost information, or data technology. In general, trade secret protection is broader and longer, but less defensible.

The main requirement for establishing a trade secret is to make a concerted effort to protect, or keep secret, the idea. What you get is protection from theft or unauthorized leakage. If someone copies your business through no creative or investigative effort of their own, but by taking your ideas or capturing key information illegally, it can be challenged in court. "Concerted effort to protect" means making some provision to retain the information. The most frequent manifestation of trade secret protection is requiring other business associates, including suppliers and key customers, to sign a Non-Disclosure Agreement or NDA, setting forth terms of disclosure and making the associate generally aware they are dealing with a trade secret. Intellectual property attorneys advise anyone with business ideas to protect them from the very start, and sign NDAs with those privy to the idea or who have knowledge that might be used in the business.

THE MAIN REQUIREMENT FOR ESTABLISHING A TRADE SECRET IS TO MAKE A CONCERTED EFFORT TO PROTECT, OR KEEP SECRET THE IDEA. WHAT YOU GET IS PROTECTION FROM THEFT OR UNAUTHORIZED LEAKAGE.

While the protection afforded by "trade secret" means is less rigorous, it does offer key advantages.

- *Indefinite.* Whereas a patent expires in 20 years, trade secret protection is forever.
- *Cheap and relatively easy to establish.* Make the effort to protect information, including NDAs and secure storage of key business information, and you should be able to get some protection.
- *Applies to almost anything.* Whereas patent and trademark protection must meet very specific criteria, almost anything can be considered a trade secret.
- *Good preparation for a patent.* Specific ideas and methods guarded as trade secrets may eventually mature into patentable ideas.
- *Good business practice.* "Loose lips sink ships," and free sharing of business ideas and knowledge usually leads to loss somewhere downstream. Successful business owners have the discipline to protect valuable information—and require others around them to do the same.

The most famous "trade secret" is the formula for Coca-Cola. Efforts to protect this secret are legendary: Supposedly only two people know the formula and they are required to always travel separately. If someone stole the formula or it leaked from one of the two confidants, Coke would have legal recourse. This protection has lasted over a century, while a patent would have lasted (then) for only 17 years. This example also illustrates the major downside of trade secret protection however: If someone duplicated the Coke formula *on their own*, in their own lab and with their own investigation, there would be no trade secret protection; a patented recipe or formula would have been protected.

Patenting Your Business Idea

Now you "know the ropes" at least to some extent. But the key question remains: Should you pursue patent or trademark protection for your niche business? It depends on your assessment of the originality and patentability of the business concept. And don't forget trademarks—it feels good to have at least *something* protected. If you're in doubt, consult an expert. You should at least consider getting the process rolling, even if you choose not to follow through later. If your idea is truly patentable and you *don't* do it, you may be sorry later. It's all about the *upside potential* of getting the protection and the *downside risk* of not getting it; these must be weighed against the cost of starting and perhaps completing the process. If you do pursue intellectual property protection, make sure you do it right and budget for professional assistance. Otherwise, what may seem to preserve value may in fact not.

A Practical Matter

Sacramento intellectual property attorney Kim Mueller advises any prospective entrepreneur, particularly one with a new business concept or idea, *at an absolute minimum* to consult with an intellectual property attorney early in the game. For a modest one-hour consultation and a few hundred dollars, you are set on a path to find the right protection for your ideas, starting with trade secret protection and—if warranted—going further. "An ounce of protection is worth many pounds of cure," says Kim. It is much easier and cheaper to take the necessary steps to protect intellectual property up front. Establishing protection later, after the product or service is already on the market, is much more difficult and often requires extensive legal effort with an uncertain outcome. Kim finds that trade secret protection is often enough, and advises her clients on how to best achieve

> ANY PROSPECTIVE ENTREPRENEUR, PARTICULARLY ONE WITH A NEW BUSINESS CONCEPT OR IDEA, SHOULD CONSULT WITH AN INTELLECTUAL PROPERTY ATTORNEY EARLY IN THE GAME.

that protection. Many intellectual property attorneys specialize in trade secret and intellectual property protection *strategy* and often charge lower rates than a fully qualified patent attorney. Just as a professional financial planner can offer broad personal finance advice and reference to more specific services for, say, estate planning, the intellectual property attorney provides protection strategy and the tools to get started before engaging the heavy artillery.

SUMMARY FOR CHAPTER 8

❖ As you develop a niche business, it is important to consider protecting intellectual property. An ounce of prevention is worth a pound of cure.

❖ Patents protect inventions. Utility patents protect the form and substance of an invention, while design patents protect the exterior appearance only.

❖ Patents provide the most defensible protection but require the most effort and cost. New patents last 20 years.

❖ Patents protect methods, machines, manufactures, and compositions. Business ideas may or may not be patentable.

❖ To be patentable, an invention must also be useful, new, and non-obvious.

❖ Provisional patents ("patent pending") provide a legal place-holder, but a patent filing must occur within one year of commercializing the invention.

❖ Trademarks protect the words, phrases, or symbols used to bring an idea to the marketplace. They need not be registered but registration provides greater protection and is cheaper and easier than getting a patent.

❖ Trade secret protection protects against theft or unauthorized use of business ideas or knowledge. It is established by making a concerted effort to protect the ideas or knowledge, as with non-disclosure agreements. Trade secret protection is broader and longer (forever) but less defensible.

❖ A short planning session with an intellectual property attorney is recommended to map out an intellectual property strategy early in the formation of a business.

Well, clearly if I get this evening care center and camp off the ground, it may have a name worth protecting. Some special activities or entertainment ideas may be protectable, but I doubt it. At the very least, I will make sure to keep any business discussions as confidential as possible; the last thing I want to see is three people opening the same business before or just after I do!

9

Will You Ever Get Noticed?

N ow, just how will I get the word out? Newspaper advertising may be expensive, untargeted, and not all that good. Knowing the newspapers, they'll place my ad just above the Purple Velvet girlie club. I need to get to those parents—the ones who work hard and need time off the most and are willing to pay. How can I get my business noticed without spending a boatload of money…?

"Publicity, that's the way to go," says Francine Krause, the founder of Pregnant Bellymasks™. When Francine first began marketing her kits she thought the world would beat a path to her door. At least she thought pregnant women would beat a path to her door. Bellymasks are kits for making plaster casts to celebrate a woman's swelling tummy. "But no one knew that when I first began trying to sell them," says Francine. "I paid a graphic artist to design a poster for my product, and hung the posters and passed out flyers in my neighborhood." Francine waited confidently for the phone to begin ringing. And waited, and waited.... Expensive advertisements in parenting magazines and newsletters didn't help either.

Francine's first real break didn't come until she put together an art show in a local gallery that featured the beautifully decorated belly masks. She phoned the local paper to let them know about it, and the result was a large article with color photos. This spawned articles in the San Francisco paper, which then lead to ones in national magazines and television coverage. "*USA Today, The Wall Street Journal, People* magazine, I've even been mentioned in the *National Enquirer!*" says Francine. Each one of these publicity hits gives her business a boost: The *People* magazine article generated 400 orders for her $65 kits in just a few short weeks.

Advertising is a basic cost of doing business. And it's a very high cost. If your new niche business needs to advertise to get clients—

PRESS COVERAGE IS LINKED: LOCAL COVERAGE LEADS TO REGIONAL AND NATIONAL COVERAGE.

if that is the only way for you to get your message out to the folks who are your potential clients—get ready to spend. And spend. And spend some more.

Publicity, on the other hand, is free. For the price of a postage stamp you can send out a press release that could generate an onslaught of free publicity. Publicity also provides you a third party endorsement of sorts. A potential customer who sees an ad for your business in which you describe it as "the best of its kind!" knows you are making that claim for yourself and is rightly cynical about whether it is true. Someone who reads a newspaper article about your business saying it is "the best of its kind!" trusts the impartial assessment of the reporter. You've done that in your own life, haven't you? Perhaps you've spotted a splashy advertisement for a cool-sounding restaurant, but not acted on the information until you read a great review in a newspaper. It is human nature to want to get in on the action, and when you read about something in a newspaper or magazine, or see a story on the television news, we want to be a part of it, too. Buy the product, eat the food, visit the hotel. Publicity sells.

> PUBLICITY IS FREE AND MAY BE BETTER THAN ADVERTISING. READERS TRUST THE IMPARTIAL ASSESSMENT OF THE MEDIA.

Advertising is a budget item in your business plan, the one you'll soon be working on in Chapter 10. To get the big picture on how much a business can spend on advertising, take a look at two eye-popping figures: $160.9 million and $149 million. In a recent news story about the proposed merger between computer makers

Hewlett-Packard and Compaq, those figures were given as the yearly ad budgets for the two companies, respectively. *Yearly* figures! That is how much they pay for the advertising they hope will both sell their products and further their brand names in the public mind. The massive media coverage of the proposed merger let the business world know about it but, didn't cost the companies much more than the paper for the press release. That was publicity, not advertising.

In the early 1990s, computer game company Electronic Arts developed their own method of valuing publicity. Their publicity department would diligently measure the actual column inches devoted to articles about the company's game products, and assign dollar value to the total using the going rate for advertising in the same publication. For instance, an article about Electronic Arts in *The Wall Street Journal* would be evaluated based on how much it would have cost them to buy an advertisement of that same size. If you look at it this way, the free publicity you can generate for your niche business can be worth hundreds of thousands of dollars a year.

What Works?

Flip through any newspaper or magazine and you will see stories about small business people. *How come they wrote about that guy?* you might ask yourself, and *Will anyone ever write a big story about me and my business?* Getting publicity and media coverage is no mystery once you know the methods. Believing that you will get the publicity you deserve will also come once you realize how it all works. So, why you? What is the media looking for?

Drum roll, please.... Here is what every newspaper reporter, magazine writer, and television talk show producer is looking for: *a story that will connect with their readers and viewers.* Whether it connects emotionally, or because the information is useful, media folks are always on the lookout for material that will keep the audience coming back for more in the next day's newspaper, next month's magazine, or tomorrow's TV show.

Why would anyone write about you? It seems hopeless...so many businesses are out there looking to be covered; will they ever choose you as a story subject? The odds are better than you think. The media is always trolling for stories, and hungry for more, more, more new and original content to satisfy their audience.

> THE MEDIA IS ALWAYS TROLLING FOR STORIES, AND HUNGRY FOR MORE NEW ORIGINAL CONTENT TO SATISFY THEIR AUDIENCE.

Imagine this: On a daily newspaper, a reporter's job doesn't end when they finish up a great story for the next day's edition. No, they have to have many things in the works for the next day's story, and the day after that, and the week after that. With a magazine, putting together the perfect December issue doesn't mean you can go home and rest for a few weeks. You have to start working on the next edition, right away. Writers, editors, and producers are under the same constant need for material. The same writers, editors, and producers that you are pitching now may end up at another company some day and remember you and your story. Francine and her Bellymasks have benefited several times from writers who've moved around a bit. "I was scheduled to be covered in *People* magazine once and then the story was canceled," says Francine. "But the writer never forgot me. The same thing happened with *Parenting* magazine." Don't ever feel shy about offering yourself

---

SPEAK UP!

The phone rings one afternoon and it's a newspaper reporter on the line, responding to a press release you just sent out. Of course you are thrilled, but your throat feels dry, your hands get clammy and your heart seems to beat so loud that you fear the reporter might ask about that annoying thumping sound. Dealing with the media can be an intimidating experience and not everyone feels comfortable promoting themselves and their business. Laurie Rood found a way to overcome her fears and reluctance: She joined a local chapter of Toastmasters International and began to build her confidence and public speaking skills.

"The more I stand up and speak before a room full of people, the easier it gets to publicize my business," she says. "I used to hate talking to the press, but now I'm pretty comfortable. I know that comfort level comes directly from Toastmasters." You can find out about Toastmasters by visiting their Web site at www.toastmasters.org.

---

and your business up as a story idea; understand that *you are exactly what they need*. Almost exactly, anyway. Here's a closer look at the actual kinds of stories that will catch the eye of the media.

Hooks and Angles

If you are building a niche business, chances are you will have a built-in hook or angle to your business. Pizza is pizza, unless it is a niche business that only sells vegetarian pizzas. A dress shop is just that, unless it only sells one color of dress—red.

Here's a great example of a niche business making full use of publicity. Specialty mountain bike store owners Richard and Kathleen Amneus of Grants Pass, Oregon, planned to leave their longtime store location and move to a newer building on the other side of town. Instead of packing up, trucking across town, and leaving a "We've Moved" sign taped to their old location, Richard and Kathleen devised a publicity plan that not only helped save on moving costs, but also rewarded their longtime customers by making them feel a part of something special. And it landed them on the front page of their local newspaper.

Weeks before the planned day of the move they began to let their customers know about it. They also said they'd love to have help. And they alerted the news media to what they had up their sleeve. On the appointed day a huge crew of folks young and old turned out in the parking lot of the store, waiting for their role to begin. Richard and Kathleen let each one choose a brand new bike and jump on; then in colorful parade formation they all rode across town to the new location. Presto! The entire stock was moved in 30 minutes, and it made for a great news story on television and in the paper. Imagine how much it would have cost to take out newspaper and TV advertisements to get the same kind of attention.

Success Is Cheap

In Chapter 2 you read about two travel agents who'd carved out their own niches in the business: Laurie Battiston built a business catering to honeymooners, and Helena Koenig built one organizing trips for grandparents to take with their grandkids. In the early '90s Jennifer carved off a tiny niche in the travel business as well. After the success of her first niche publishing project, *The Sacramento*

Women's Yellow Pages, she expanded to publish a book that catered to budget travelers. It was for hard core budget travelers, the kind who didn't want to pay more than a few hundred dollars to fly someplace exotic. Jennifer learned about how air couriers can fly overseas for a fraction of the price of a ticket. The result was a small booklet, *The Air Courier's Handbook,* aimed at this special niche of flexible, budget-conscious travelers. She sold 5,000 copies in five years with just a few hundred dollars invested in stationery, envelopes, and stamps.

How did Jennifer do this? Twice a year she would undertake a publicity campaign to travel editors of magazines and newspapers. In the early years she worried that no one would write about her tiny booklet, but they did. Major newspapers like the *Boston Globe,* *LA Times,* and *Chicago Tribune* took up the story, as did regional papers in small towns all over the country. *Cosmopolitan* magazine wrote about *The Air Courier's Handbook* not once, but twice. In the first few months after publication Jennifer did try a few small ads in travel magazines, but quickly abandoned the effort once she saw how easy it was to get publicity. Why did all of these jaded travel editors write about her booklet? It was quirky and offbeat and exciting, and the only one of its kind. It was a perfectly profitable niche.

How can you assess the publicity potential of your niche business? Every business has a natural and special path to publicity, and you can learn how to create it. Just as there are ways to spin a fascinating tale from the ordinary things that happen in our lives, it is possible to put a more colorful spin on you, your business, and even the niche that you serve. Helena Koenig has a great hook with her travel business Grandtravel. The idea behind the business is intriguing enough, but imagine how much more media interest she can generate when she lets travel editors know some of the details from trips. These are stories of grandparents taking the grandchildren to exotic spots around the world, and the amusing anecdotes that happen along the way. It is all in the telling.

Publicity Potential Assessment

Here is a list of questions to get you pondering your future publicity potential:

- ❖ Is your new business the only one of its kind in the area?
- ❖ Do you have a colorful background?
- ❖ Can you stage an event, or a series of events, around your business?
- ❖ Does your business tie into current events or news stories?
- ❖ Is there media that targets your niche audience?
- ❖ Is your business humorous in any way?
- ❖ Is there more than one story that can be generated about your business?

Is Your New Business the Only One of its Kind in the Area?

The first business in any new category is the one that gets the most media coverage. If you are the first chimney sweep in your area you stand a chance of a story; you don't if you are the fifth. If there are already similar businesses in your niche you might need to reassess your idea, not only for the publicity potential, but also whether the niche is large enough to support more than one business. What's your worst scenario? It's when there is another niche business just like the one you want to start, and it's one that has already received tons of media coverage. Stay away!

Do You Have a Colorful Background?

If your business itself is dull (and some niche businesses are!) perhaps your own background makes an interesting angle. Is there an interesting story behind the founding of your business? What if it was influenced by something you saw on a round-the-world trek, such as Tibetan prayer flags. Or maybe the idea came to you one afternoon while you were daydreaming in grade school, but it took you 30 years to develop it. Are you in business with your sibling? That worked as a great hook for the two brothers that founded the job-hunting Web site Guru.com and served as co-CEOs. It helped them get their story out in an otherwise crowded niche. Sit down and try to draw up a colorful (but true) explanation for why you began your business. A large article in *The New York Times* recently featured a professor of history in Durham, North Carolina, who has a side job as an expert auto mechanic. Woe to all the worthy history professors overlooked by the *Times* because they can't handle a rear main seal job!

Can You Stage an Event, or a Series of Events, Around Your Business?

Events can create traffic and customers, spread your reputation, and bring out the media. Annual ones can help you build business and local awareness, but even one-time affairs can generate great publicity. Does your niche business lend itself to an event? Imagine the colorful events online sports equipment retailer Unicycle.com can stage. A parade of unicyclists, or a game of unicycle polo…either one would bring out the cameras. Jennifer once sent bookstore employees out onto the street corner with giant bubble wands to wave in the air. She was promoting both a soap bubble book and the store itself. A timely call to a television newsroom on a slow Sunday brought their cameramen down in no time to capture the enormous glistening bubbles floating through the air (in full view of the store's sign, of course). Why not brainstorm a list of possible events you could create around your business? The more, the merrier.

Does Your Business Tie into Current Events or News Stories?

Is there something about your niche business that is timely from a news perspective? Does it relate to a growing trend? Remember Leslie Hammond in Chapter 2; she's the woman who bakes allergy-free birthday cakes for children's parties because food allergies are on the rise. Her niche business is a perfect tie-in with something that the media will report on anyway. She happens to have a product that relates to a large health problem, as well as an emotional hook in the way she tells her story. It's perfect.

The horrific events at the World Trade Center in September 2001 shocked the nation. But the images of soot-covered evacuees created the perfect moment for manufacturers of smoke-hoods to get their message out about increasing your chances for survival in a large building fire. Equally fast-thinking was Jalem Getz, the CEO of BuyCostumes.com, who received quick publicity due to the firestorm around Congressman Gary Condit. Getz put a poll on his Web site asking if customers would wear a Halloween mask with Condit's face on it, and then released the results (16 percent said the idea was lousy) to the media. Think about how your business can be tied into news events and always be ready to spring into action whenever the opportunity arises.

Is There Media that Targets Your Niche Audience?

Does your niche market have its own newspaper or magazine? For example, there is *The Senior Times* for businesses that target older folks, and *Dog Fancy* for those that target pet owners. Draw up a list of all of the magazines and newspapers you think might write about your new business, and jot down why you think they will cover you. *The Senior Times* will probably write about a business that installs walkways and ramps for wheelchairs, not about one that doesn't have a compelling angle of interest to their readers. If your niche doesn't have its own media, is there a section in the newspaper that targets it? Perhaps the food, the travel, or music and entertainment section would be a fit. If you can't think of a single place that an article about your business might appear, you might be headed for trouble.

Is Your Business Humorous in any Way?

Businesses with a humorous twist, like Bone Appetit, a bakery that makes treats for dogs, are always easy to get free publicity for. "So much of what reporters write about isn't funny. Crime, war, business failures…they welcome an opportunity to write something more light-hearted and humorous," says publicist Robin Lockwood. "Irony also works." Flip through the pages of *People* magazine and you'll notice how many of their short pieces on entrepreneurs have a humorous or wacky angle. A funny business might not get you noticed by *Fortune* or *Forbes*, but it will help just about everywhere else.

Is There More than One Story that Can be Generated about Your Business?

Ideally you will be able to generate publicity throughout the life of your business, above and beyond the initial burst when you first open up. Is there potential for more than one story? Now that you have considered the questions above, you should have a long list. You should also be able to put together a colorful story about who you are and why you opened this business, think of a good way to tie into current events as they occur, craft a humorous story to catch the media's interest, and create event after event that will draw attention on a large scale. You want to be able to pitch yourself and your business over and over again in many different ways; this will keep the publicity stream rushing your way.

PUBLICITY COUP

The financial services business is a crowded one, with stockbrokers, money managers, and financial analysts all vying to receive publicity from the most important source of all—*The Wall Street Journal*. This well-known industry newspaper is besieged on a daily basis with press releases and story ideas from folks in the financial community who know the kind of boost they'd get from even a small mention on its pages. With so many credentialled experts lurking, why would *The Journal* devote a large front page story to a woman who had only had her stockbroker's license for three years, and opened her business, Native Nations Securities Inc., in 1999? Because she had an incredible niche business. Valerie Red-Horse saw the need for a securities firm controlled by an American Indian. What was her target market? American Indian tribal organizations. Many Native American Indian tribes now have enormous amounts of ready cash due to gambling operations, lawsuit settlements, and other far-flung business interests. Red-Horse's competitors in this emerging market are large banks like Bank of America and major financial services companies, but with her heritage she clearly has an inside edge on both the business and the publicity.

Media Stardom

Does every entrepreneur seek media stardom? Of course not; and many of those who seek it fall short. How can national media possibly help your small town business? If the niche business you plan to create will only serve one geographic area, what good could come out of a feature in *USA Today* or a mention in the *Chicago Tribune*? Plenty.

When assessing your publicity potential and drawing up your media plans, think about the possible benefits of national publicity. Even if you plan to operate your niche business in one geographic location, national publicity might bring you folks who want to franchise your business idea. Don't want to get into franchising? Then draw up a solid business plan that can be duplicated and sell it for a one-time charge. Years ago an enterprising woman got major publicity for a doggy doo removal business she operated and ended up selling plans to folks all around the country. She also sold them the special "doo-doo-picker-upper" she'd designed.

Other opportunities that could present themselves after a burst of publicity include increased media attention in your hometown (now that you have received national publicity you are indeed a *star*), and the potential that you might be approached by other folks with business ideas who want you to be their partner.

Publicity begets publicity. "I can trace the history of some of my publicity," says Francine Krause of Pregnant Bellymasks™. "*People* magazine found me in *The Wall Street Journal*. *USA Today* found me in *Parenting* magazine, who'd found me in the *San Francisco Examiner*." And so it goes, from one media outlet to the next.

Perfecting Your Pitch

Remember, you want lots and lots of publicity for your niche business. So let's start learning how to "pitch" yourself and your business in ways that will attract media attention. Using the example of Unicycle.com, let's see how John and Amy Drummond could easily craft several different types of media pitches tailored to various audiences.

❖ *Local newspaper.* John could pitch his local newspaper a story about how he left his lifelong career with IBM in order to fulfill this longing to be an entrepreneur. He decided to sell unicycles when he realized how hard it was to replace the one he'd been riding since his teens.

❖ *Morning radio show.* The quirky flavor of drive-time radio requires a light-hearted approach. John and Amy could let the radio station give away a unicycle to a caller who came up with the best suggestion for what a unicyclist could be doing with their free hands while riding—perhaps holding a newspaper, drinking coffee, or using a cell phone.

❖ *National newspaper.* In addition to the story behind the founding and success of Unicycle.com, John and Amy could use a health angle to interest a national newspaper. Studies have shown that the unicycle gives riders a better full body workout than a bicycle does.

❖ *National television show.* A story could be a combination of several of the above ideas, with the added flavor of actually showing a group of unicyclists in action. A parade of unicyclists makes a great visual, which is something television needs in order to work.

Spend some time trying to come up with similar ways to position your business to different types of media. Try crazy ideas, or more modest ones, until you get a better sense of how to catch the media's eye.

Still not able to come up with any great ideas to pitch your business? Subscribe to the online e-zine *Publicity Hound* and receive their weekly tips. You'll soon be coming up with an idea a week. Sign up at www.publicityhound.com. Another good Web site and newsletter with publicity information and tips is www.prsecrets. com. It's run by media coach and marketing expert Susan Harrow, author of *Sell Yourself without Selling Your Soul*.

The Oprah Factor

Every author now knows what a career launcher an appearance on Oprah was, and many an entrepreneur felt Oprah's golden touch, too. Her show is now scheduled to end in 2005, so you'll have to move quickly if that's your goal! Would a large television show ever be interested in you and your business? Maybe…here is what Susan Harrow says about how to position yourself for Oprah-like success: "Pitch a hot topic. Never pitch yourself or your product. Instead pitch something that is newsworthy: a pressing national issue, a controversial subject, a problem for which you have the solution, or a common myth debunked. Propose a topic that is relevant to the show's audience (controversy, relationships, personal triumph, makeovers) and then prove that you are the expert on that topic."

Are you ready to approach the show once you've got your angle figured out? No. Susan believes there is yet more work to be done. "Tape the show," she says. Part of preparing for success is becoming familiar with the content, rhythm, and pace of the show. Tape two to four weeks, and then sit down to watch them all at once. This will give you a solid sense of what's hot for the next few months. Notice which producers (listed in the credits that roll over the screen at the end) are responsible for which type of segment. Send a producer information only after you are sure of whom you'd like to approach and why." Follow Harrow's advice to the letter, and you, too may soon be settling in on the couch next to a talk show host.

Events Galore

You read earlier about staging events as a way to create publicity. Even a small-scale event can be a powerful way to draw attention to your niche business. But if you are at a loss for ideas about what would work, why not get together with other businesses to create something larger? A quick glance at a recent food section from our local California newspaper mentioned to several regional food

PRESS RELEASE BASICS

In order to catch the media's eye (or ear) you'll need to learn how to write a press release. This is a one-page announcement sent to various members of the media. It serves to catch the interest of the person reading it—and catch it fast. "You have to get their attention right away, in the first few words," counsels professional publicist Robin Lockwood. "And just as important, you have to get it to the right editor. Call the publication to make sure they are still there, and get the proper spelling of their name."

Press releases begin with a catchy headline. The same one will often be used in newspaper and magazine articles, so choose carefully.

The following are two press release headlines that Pregnant Bellymasks might use to hook an editor's interest:

- Creating Art from Life's Most Wondrous Moment
- Popular Craft Takes off at Baby Showers

Each of these was crafted to jolt a jaded reporter or editor into responding and asking you for more information. How can you create art from life's most wondrous moment? An editor would keep reading to find out. What popular craft is being done at baby showers? A reporter would read on to learn what it was. Make sure you are encouraging your target audience (the media) to keep reading.

A press release needs to deliver the basic five Ws: who, what, where, why, and when. And you need to be clear about your purpose: Are you trying to interest the reader in a news story? Are you announcing a press conference or new store opening? Be clear about the purpose of your release.

festivals that were planned; they included everything from a cheese-tasting contest in Modesto to an eggplant festival in Loomis and a tomato festival in the Carmel Valley. No one businessperson planned these events; instead they are the product of a coalition of like-minded people who sat down and thought, How can we draw attention to what we do, create a crowd, and make some money?

Building the Buzz

In addition to soliciting free publicity, you might also want to consider building a bit of buzz around your business. Will it be able to

> WORD OF MONTH HAS ACHIEVED TREMENDOUS RESULTS IN THE PAST; HOW
> DO YOU THINK ALL THOSE KIDS ON THE PLAYGROUND FOUND OUT ABOUT
> POKÉMON?

benefit from word-of-mouth marketing? Word-of-mouth has achieved tremendous results in the past; how do you think all of those kids on the playground found out about Pokémon? They heard it from other kids on the playground.

In order to build buzz around your business you will need to be able to tap into the influential folks in your niche audience. Find the trend builders and get them talking about you. During a recent product launch of Pox, a handheld game for boys, the manufacturer asked ordinary kids who they thought was the coolest kid in their school. Once they had a collection of "cool kids" from across the country, the toy maker gave those kids free samples of Pox and began teaching them how to play the game. What a way to spread the word! Could you do this with your new business—get in touch with the opinion makers and give them free samples or an early, inside look at what you are planning? Sharing product, giving tours of your business before it opens, and sending out samples are all ways to build buzz and anticipation. Just remember: Buzz works both ways. Influential folks could build your business if they love what you do; they could also ruin you if they are less than impressed and begin talking about that.

Sounds Too Good

Publicity sounds like exactly what you need to make your business take off like a rocket. Is there a downside to it? Can it ever hurt your business? Yes, it can.

Picture this: A large and flattering newspaper story appears about your niche product, making it sound so swell that your phone begins to ring off the hook with orders. However, there is one problem: Your product isn't ready yet. All of those enthusiastic callers are now disappointed, and may never call again.

Publicity can hit too early, before your product is ready or your store is open. This can do real damage by creating unhappy customers or a media unwilling to write about you later on (when you are ready).

How can you avoid these scenarios? Make sure you are completely prepared to handle any response *before* you send out a press release. Publicity can be a godsend once you understand how to harness it. Put all these tricks to work as you plan your business, and you are well on your way to understanding how to "niche and grow rich"!

Now that you have a better sense of how to assess the publicity potential of your business idea, and how to start generating that powerful publicity even before you open your doors, let's get back to basics. How do you open those doors? Yes, you know how to use a key…but these are some other helpful keys to make sure that once you open those doors, they stay open! Read Chapter 10 to learn more about successfully opening your niche business.

SUMMARY FOR CHAPTER 9

❖ Advertising costs, but publicity is free.

❖ Publicity is not only free, but an unbiased, third party endorsement of your business.

❖ The media constantly looks for stories that connect emotionally with their audience. Remember, they need content, and you need publicity.

❖ The specialty and uniqueness of a niche business is usually more attractive to the media than a "mainstream" business.

❖ Publicity potential is highest if
  – you're the first business of your kind in the area
  – you have a colorful background
  – you can stage events around your business
  – the business ties with current events, news stories, or areas of popular interest (conservation, energy efficiency)
  – there is targeted media for your audience (senior gazette)
  – the business is humorous or funny (bone appetit)
  – more than one story can be generated about the business

❖ Remember: publicity begets publicity

❖ You can get assistance on publicity strategy and placement through professional coaches, publicists, and a few Web sites

❖ Press releases are an effective publicity tool

❖ Never forget the power of word-of-mouth publicity

Oh, I get it now! Get written up in the newspaper for free! Yes, this is a new enough idea with broad interest; I just bet a reporter would take it up. And maybe an open house? A partnership with local day care centers to exchange business? Flyers in restaurants (yes, they're interested too, because they want to get these parents out just as much as these parents want to get out—on some evening other than Saturday!). Gosh, the creative wheels are turning fast now....

10

Basic Steps for Opening a Niche Business

*A*ll systems are still "go." You've committed to a business idea you're pretty sure will fly. You feel good about the market potential. You've looked into protecting the idea, and you're comfortable that you have the know-how and resources to get started. The next step is to "lock and load" — begin the final planning and implementation steps necessary to actually get going.

In a sense starting the niche business is as simple as starting a school yard race: *get ready*, *get set*, and *go*.

* ❖ *"Get ready"* means finalizing and documenting a design blue-print and business plan for the business. Business plans are vital for (1) clarifying and focusing your thinking around *exactly what the business is* and *how it will work*, and (2) pre-senting the concept to financial backers and others you need for the launch. The specific details and template for creating a business plan are beyond the scope of this book, but you'll learn some of the highlights and major components that are important to address.

* ❖ *"Get set"* refers to the pre-launch preparation necessary to actually open the business. The business plan contains mar-keting, operational, and financial components. In the "get set" stage, you lay the foundation and begin executing these pieces of the plan. Agreements must be made, networks established, locations chosen, people hired and trained, visual images and advertising created, data management processes established, legal documents prepared, and financial resources obtained.

* ❖ *"Go"* refers to actually launching the business. Announce-ments, publicity, trial offers, and special marketing programs to introduce your product/service to the niche all happen here.

Why Is a Plan Important?

Since we're talking "niche" business here, it is important to go through these steps. Financial backers will want to understand your niche and get comfortable with your potential success in it. In *Pour Your Heart Into It*, Howard Schultz, founder and chairman of

Starbucks, speaks of the difficulties of attracting financial and other kinds of backing for his *then* new idea. Many business people take the conservative view and invest only in proven concepts. Your niche idea may well be excellent, or it may appear speculative and unproven. And if your product or service tries to fill a niche but misses, you may wind up with a specialized product or service that has no market; then the seeds of failure sprout. Your homework assignment as a niche entrepreneur is to dispel these concerns with a solid, documented story. The three "C's" of starting a niche business are: *clarity, clarity, clarity.*

THE THREE "C'S" OF STARTING A NICHE BUSINESS ARE CLARITY, CLARITY, CLARITY.

The Essential Business Plan

"Essential" is the key word here. Business plans can be simple five-page jobs or elaborate, picture- and graph-laden book-size documents. If you're planning to start a large business, particularly one with plans to go to the public capital markets, you're probably looking at a book-size version. But many small niche entrepreneurships can be documented and clarified in short and simple form. Greater brevity forces clear, crisp thought, and that's a good thing.

Business Planning Resources

Sometimes the hardest part of writing or documenting *anything* is determining what to write *about* and how to structure it. Fortunately, the business reference bookshelf provides ample literature on structuring and writing business plans. These books provide recipes and examples that allow you to focus on *content*. Guides to business and marketing planning are numerous. Three of the best are:

1. *The Successful Business Plan* by Rhonda Abrams (Running "R" Media)
2. *Business Plans Made Easy Second Edition* by Mark Henricks and John Riddle (Entrepreneur Press)
3. *Preparing the Marketing Plan* by David Parmerlee (NTC Business Books)

These books all take a practical approach, giving forms, templates, examples, checklists, sample tables, graphics, and advice. They are readily available at most bookstores. It is essential, enlightening, and even fun to wrap your business idea around one of these planning templates.

Many Web sites also provide useful tools, templates, and advice for the entrepreneur. Entrepreneur.com is a good example. You'll find almost everything you need there; it's like one-stop shopping for business plan information. The U.S. Small Business Administration ("America's Small Business Resource") also has a wide range of "getting started" advice and materials, including a free, downloadable business planning outline and template. See www.sba.gov, and more specifically, www.sba.gov/starting.

For a deeper view of how to develop a business plan and idea within specific industries or business types, Entrepreneur Press provides a set of "Start-Up Guides." These are available for over 40 different business types, from consulting to restaurants to child care to starting your own herb farm. They augment the conventional business planning guides by giving business-specific evaluation criteria and advice from experienced entrepreneurs. A complete list is available at Entrepreneur Books (www.smallbiz books.com).

What's In a Business Plan?

Business plans should contain at least three parts: a *marketing plan*, an *operating plan*, and a *financial plan*. Each part focuses on the critical elements that make your niche business clear, unique, and successful. It also addresses contingencies, or the *what-if's* for when things don't turn out exactly as planned. The business plan outlines specific resource requirements needed to make features of the marketing, operating, and financial plans *work*. These can be financial resources, but also human resources, professional services, data and information, or external or "environmental" factors required to make *your* business a success.

The Marketing Plan

Many elements of the marketing plan in Chapter 6 "Six Steps to Evaluating a Niche". The marketing plan *defines* the market: who it is, how big it is, and how the product/service meets its needs. Then the plan describes how the product will be brought to market. This is where you encounter the four elements, or "Ps," of the market mix: product, price, promotion, and place (physical distribution). This is what most people think of as the marketing plan. Product definition, pricing, discounts, packaging, advertising, promotional ideas, and distribution channels must all be addressed. Finally, the plan should identify sales and growth potential. "How big is the market" must be turned into dollars—sales dollars—both now and in the future, to determine if market size is sufficient to support a business. The sales forecast connects the marketing plan to the operational and financial plans (see Figure 10.1).

FIGURE 10.1 Elements of the Marketing Plan

Market definition

- Target market
- Key customers
- Market size
- How product/service meets needs

Marketing mix

- Product definition, assortment, packaging
- Pricing discounts, add-ons
- Promotion and advertising
- Physical distribution, how and where the product is sold

Sales forecast

- Projected sales volume and dollars
- Future growth paths

Again, this is a simplistic, "bottom line" overview. A detailed marketing plan will elaborate on many of these points and add others. Business-to-business marketing plans contain the same basic elements as a business-to-consumer plan, but may place more emphasis on key customers and the sales process. A concise, clearly stated plan that addresses all of the above elements in clear and understandable detail will help focus your thoughts and be useful

THE MARKETING PLAN DEFINES THE MARKET AND DESCRIBES HOW A PRODUCT OR SERVICE WILL BE BROUGHT TO IT.

to you and others touched by your business. It also provides vital ingredients necessary for the rest of your business recipe: the operating and financial plans.

The Operating Plan

The operating plan talks about *how* your business plan—especially your marketing plan—will be implemented. It is the *how* part that doesn't talk about money. (That privilege is reserved for the financial plan.) While the marketing plan is mainly strategy with a few tactics (like advertising plans), the operating plan is more about tactics. Operating plans may be simple, as for a homebased writing business, or elaborate and detailed, as for a manufacturing business or a business requiring a large number of employees.

Many key strategic decisions need to be made to successfully start and operate a business. These fall into three categories: location, production, and human resources (see Figure 10.2).

> THE OPERATING PLAN EXPLAINS HOW YOUR BUSINESS WILL OPERATE TO ACHIEVE THE MARKETING PLAN. IT INCLUDES A LOCATION PLAN, PRODUCTION PLAN, AND HUMAN RESOURCES PLAN.

Location Plan. You've heard it before in real estate: The three things to look for are location, location, and location. Depending on the niche business you want to create, this cliché can also apply to you. If customer traffic is important, you need to locate where the customers—the right ones—are. If you're selling equipment and supplies for water sports, it might be a good idea to locate near water, or *on the way* to it. Picking the right location is an art and a science;

FIGURE 10.2 Elements of the Operating Plan

Location plan
- Proximity to market
- Visibility
- Cost

Production plan
- Manufacturing process
- Service process
- Outsourcing
- Suppliers
- Delivery
- Costs

Human resources plan
- How much help
- What kind of help
- When—what time of day or year
- Professional and other services

it requires tradeoff of proximity to market and visibility, against the cost.

Location decisions may also depend on factors beyond proximity to markets; cost and production factors can be important. Cost factors include those of doing business, such as obtaining the location, taxes, transportation, and labor. Production factors include the availability of labor and other key procured supply inputs. For instance, it may not be wise to locate a fresh orange juice-based drinks company in Alaska.

The best locations are usually the most expensive. For the niche entrepreneur with a location-sensitive business, it may be important to locate *near your niche*—not necessarily where most of the population travels, but *where your niche* travels. What you really must think through is (1) how important the location is to the success of your business, and (2) *how much* are you willing to pay to get a better location. Making the decision requires anything from ordinary common sense to formal (and expensive) geographic location studies done by business consultants. The Small Business Administration offers resources to help with location planning, and if you're pursuing the franchising track, many franchisors provide extensive help and may have already done location studies to determine the size and viability of a market in an area.

Another thing to remember is that location isn't always about physical real estate. Web-based businesses need to "locate" themselves in the right places, on the right portals, and linked to the right sites. This also costs money, and can make or break a niche e-business. This idea overlaps with the marketing plan—the publicity, promotion and advertising components—but it is important enough to reinforce here.

Don't overlook the power of co-location. You can take a page from big business on this one. For example, large companies like Allied Doniq make sure their Baskin Robbins stores are co-located (share the same premises) with Subway sandwich shops. Can you co-locate your business with another one in a way that makes

> DON'T OVERLOOK THE POWER OF CO-LOCATION.

sense? Perhaps you could put your hip juice bar in the back of a skate and surf shop, or rent space for your adventure travel company from a larger camping equipment store.

Production Plan. This varies greatly depending on what your niche product is. If it's a technologically complex physical product, you will need to identify where it will be produced, how, and for how much. For services, "features" determined in the marketing plan will have to be converted to processes and production needs. How will the service be delivered? What kind of people, how many, and what kind of communication and data system will be required to make sure customer needs are met? Production plans also include sourcing plans, whether you're buying finished products to distribute or deliver or making a product from raw materials. Where will you get products or raw materials? Who are the suppliers? What are the lead times? What about prices and terms? Should you outsource the production or delivery? To whom? It's a good idea to identify these before getting started. And oh, by the way, if you're about to open a business and go around and talk to a few suppliers, you might land yourself some financial help in the form of discounts, or get information or resources crucial to the marketing plan ("...glad you're starting this business. We get all sorts of calls for this service and we just can't provide it..."). Funny things happen when you talk to suppliers. Some of them may even want to sell you part of a business, grant you a special license or franchise, or give you client information. What a way to get a head start!

Assume your niche business is about delivering food; then the production plan needs to cover (1) how the food will be prepared or sourced and (2) how it will be delivered. Communications (phone system, computerized tracking, etc.), transportation (cars, bikes, parking, rush hour traffic patterns), and human resources (how many delivery people, at what times of day, what days, what time of year) would all be part of the plan.

Human Resource Plan. Human resources were just mentioned as part of the production plan in the food delivery example. But for many

---

TALKING TO SUPPLIERS:
DAVE BROWN COMMERCIAL PHOTOGRAPHY STORY

Dave Brown, the successful commercial photographer in Cincinnati, Ohio introduced in Chapter 2, specialized in aerial and industrial photography. He was looking to resign from his employer and start his own studio focused (pardon the pun) on this same niche. Dave had long been running the studio arm of one of the largest commercial photo processing firms in the city. His boss owned the firm. One day he tiptoed into his boss's office; he was ready to offer his resignation, but first wanted to line the firm up to supply professional photofinishing services. He did end up with an agreement and favorable pricing for the services, but there was a much bigger surprise in store. The owner offered to sell—and finance the purchase of—the studio at a great price since it had become a poor fit with the wholesale-oriented photofinishing business. Dave got not only a supplier, but also a turnkey business, complete with equipment and an excellent client list. Moral of the story: You never know what you might get when you talk to potential suppliers, including your old boss!

---

businesses, human resources are a key element important enough to consider separately. They are expensive and often specialized, so it's good to articulate what kind of resources are needed and where they will come from. If you're unlikely to find people "off the street" to do what your business needs, the human resource plan should include training requirements and a training plan. Of course, the human resource plan is less important for a home-based business, but don't underestimate the importance of the need to identify resources to expand capacity (when you get too busy) or provide professional services when necessary (legal, accounting, copywriting, or delivery). You'll also want to identify the cost, including salary and fees, of retaining human resources. The more clearly these are identified upfront, the less surprised you'll be later, and the fewer questions you'll get from lenders and other supporters.

The Financial Plan

This is the most crucial plan for most businesses. All the good marketing ideas and production/delivery processes in the world don't mean a thing if they aren't financially sound. Businesses only thrive if—over the long run—revenues exceed costs. The financial plan is a test of whether the business model can show revenues exceeding costs, or a *profit,* either now or eventually.

Naturally, the key elements of the financial plan are sales and revenue projections, and cost projections. An important but not-so-obvious ingredient is *time.* The question is not whether revenues exceed costs the day the business starts, but if it will *ever* achieve profitability—*enough* to justify the investment of capital and time required. These are the key questions that the financial plan seeks to answer (see Figure 10.3).

FIGURE 10.3 Elements of the Financial Plan

Revenue plan

- Sales volume
- Sales mix
- Pricing, discounts, extended dollars (net price x quantity)
- Projection of future, growth plan

Cost projection

- Cost structure
- Investment costs
- Production costs
- Operating costs

Profit plan

- Revenue less cost
- Assumptions
- Scenarios

Revenue Plan. This was discussed in Chapter 6, about sizing markets. A sales forecast is a declension from how many potential customers there *are* to how many will buy your product (or products, or services). Market size and estimates of market penetration are the key drivers.

The next step is to convert to dollars, and this is where price comes in. It's not enough to know that you'll sell 150 pizzas a week; you must also know how much they will sell for and cost to produce. What is the *mix* of sizes and numbers of toppings? How many drinks will you sell? Will there be a salad bar? How many discount coupons do you plan to give out, and at what discount? Can you still make money if every customer that walks through the door shows up with a discount coupon in hand? How many no-shows do you expect on phone orders? All of these factors go into a revenue projection, and will need to decide how precise to be. Many entrepreneurs get too detailed and try to forecast the exact quantity of every "SKU" (stock-keeping-unit, or stocked item) sold. It is better to group things in categories and apply averages; the errors will cancel out and you'll spend your time on more important things. That said, it's important to somehow arrive at a realistic revenue forecast. And of course, it goes beyond this week, month, or even year—a good one projects well into the future, perhaps three to five years.

Cost Projection. The cost projection is just as important as the revenue forecast in the overall financial plan. As dotcom entrepreneurs learned, it takes more than eyeballs and revenue dollars to build a business. Any entrepreneur—niche or otherwise—must understand costs and the *cost structure* of the business.

What does cost *structure* mean? Stopping well short of a CPA course that no one wishes to endure, it is important to understand the nature of costs encountered in your business. At the risk of oversimplifying, a cost structure consists of: investment, production, and operating.

❖ *Investment costs* are for "big ticket" asset items such as facilities, equipment, and rights and other intellectual property that must be acquired to get started. Slightly more subtle are the "working capital" requirements—the cash required for business flow-through, which can be as simple as what's in the cash drawer or complex as accounts receivable and necessary inventory investments. This "seed capital"—and its costs in the form of interest or other compensation to its providers—needs to be understood and estimated. And a certain portion of the investment must be reserved as an expense every reporting period (depreciation and amortization for you accountants) to allow for replacement.

❖ *Production costs* are the "direct" costs, also known as "cost of goods sold," incurred in producing the product or service. If you're making widgets, production costs are those for raw materials, labor, and overhead (for example, utilities and administration). Service businesses have the same costs except for those for raw materials. Revenue dollars less production costs give "gross profit" (in dollars) or "gross margin" (as a percentage); these are key indicators of business success. Gross profit dollars must pay for depreciation (the reserve to replace assets) and operating expenses; there should also be some left for profit. Don't overlook the fact that your production costs are directly driven by the volume of the product or service delivered. The more you make, the better the price you can get, and the cheaper your costs. Alas, the reverse is also true: If you are only doing a small business, your costs are more.

❖ *Operating costs* are the expenses not directly related to producing your good or service. Here's where such things as marketing, selling, and administrative expenses all fit in. Advertising costs, professional services, fees, facility maintenance costs, office supplies, and transportation costs (unless you're in the transport business) all fit here.

It will be important to project these three cost factors in aggregate and in some detail. Financial backers will want to know how much investment is required, what the gross profit potential is, and how much of that gross profit will be required for operating expenses and asset replacement. They will also want to know if you have a good "handle" on costs. A cloudy cost picture will rain on even the most secure marketing and revenue plan. You need to understand where the big cost "levers" are—what factors will make or break your business. Understanding the "break-even" point, or level of business required to cover expenses and avoid a loss, is important.

> A CLOUDY COST PICTURE WILL RAIN ON EVEN THE MOST SECURE MARKETING AND REVENUE PLAN.

Profit Plan. To create the financial plan, the revenue and cost projections are blended over a period of time to provide a profit projection. The profit plan should articulate *when* you will be profitable and *how* you will do it.

The best financial plans (1) document assumptions, as many and as well as possible, (2) build complete financial projections, including income statements, balance sheets, and cash projections, and (3) examine multiple scenarios—best-case, expected-case, and

> THE PROFIT PLAN SHOULD ARTICULATE WHEN YOU WILL BECOME PROFITABLE AND HOW YOU WILL BECOME PROFITABLE.

worst-case. Many dig further into "best-case sales, worst-case costs" and "expected-case sales, best-case costs." These scenarios allow you and your providers to understand the *possibilities*. And that's what business is all about.

Final Comments on Business Planning

❖ *It doesn't have to be perfect, just good.* A perfect business plan is impossible, and a near-perfect one will take so much of your time that you won't be able to do anything else to get your business started. The right business plan has enough clarity and foundation to get the point across (to your grandmother, banker, or whomever) without diving into unnecessary and imprecise detail.

❖ *It must be done.* Too many businesses start on a loose cognitive "understanding" of the idea, then get bogged down with "gee, I didn't think of that" contingencies. Without clear documentation and the analysis that goes into it, it's easy for a business to go off course or miss an opportunity for which it was well intended. It's important to think through a business; many people apply more diligence to a car purchase than the details of a business start-up.

❖ *A realistic business plan is especially important for a niche business.* Good planning ensures that there *is indeed* a niche and that the intended business can meet that need—*profitably.* Without a plan, a good idea may never progress beyond just that. Does anyone out there own shares in Webvan? The niche was definitely there, but there was little hope of ever serving it profitably.

In short, *do the due diligence.*

Get Set: The Start-Up Funnel

As important as business planning is, it makes no sense to have a great plan and then follow it up with poor execution. The business plan will help guide the execution, or development and launch of the business, but it doesn't do the tactical legwork. Starting a business requires carefully coordinated and managed activities around actually acquiring the resources, preparing them, and deploying them in a balanced way. Businesses that fail here will, for example, get the advertising, or even better, publicity word out but offer a busy signal or cold food when the first customers come to call. Where does that get you? Nothing will kill or seriously injure a new business like this kind of failure. The three "Ps" of getting set might be *preparation*, *preparation*, and *preparation*.

There are many books on starting businesses, and they cover everything from business planning to acquiring licenses, signing legal agreements, getting insurance, and asking for money. It's impossible to squeeze all that into this chapter. This will, however, cover the essentials of preparing a business launch: acquiring and preparing resources, building networks, establishing tracking mechanisms, getting the message ready, and identifying an exit strategy.

Acquire and Prepare Resources

Acquiring resources means getting all the marketing, operational, and financial (yes, money) resources lined up to ensure a balanced and smooth start.

> ❖ *Marketing.* The marketing resources required follow the strategy and tactics outlined in the marketing plan. Such resources include design, logos, a business name, advertising space and agreements, and distribution agreements. If you're

planning to sell your product through another distributor or retailer, you had better get an agreement—and better yet an order forecast and initial order—from that channel partner.

❖ *Operational.* You must acquire the capacity to produce the product or service. Leases, purchases, rentals, and outsourcing agreements all come into play. Make sure you acquire what you need, and that you have an idea what additional resources you could get your hands on and at what price. Your idea may be better than you think and you don't want to disappoint customers by failing to deliver. Negative word of mouth can be very destructive. Where substantial up-front resource commitments must be made, know what the "exit" possibilities and costs are in case things *don't* work out.

❖ *Human.* Human resources are part of operational resources. However, they are so critical, especially to initial success, that they warrant their own mention. Once you know how many of what kind of people you need, you should spare no effort in hiring them; then make sure they're properly trained. Having the wrong people or ones who don't understand your niche or business can be destructive right out of the chute. Again, this is a surefire way to alienate customers on whom you so depend for repeat business and spreading the word. Many new business owners fail to "think through" their hiring and training plans.

❖ *Financial.* This is the big one for many businesses. Asking for money can be the most challenging—or the easiest—thing you do. If your business plan is tight and informative, financial backing should be easy to attain. What more could an investor or lender want than a business that owns a special market without competition? If your plan is convincing as to the presence of the market and the ability of your product/service to meet the need, financing should be no problem. If it isn't, be prepared to dance a bit. Investors and lenders will be doing lots of "cake tests"—sticking toothpicks in various parts of your business plan "cake" to see if things are done and thought through. If you're having trouble with financing, that's a sign the business plan may need more attention.

Build Networks

Business success, especially for small businesses is relying more and more on building effective networks. It can be prohibitively expensive, even as a niche entrepreneur, to get the word out and sustain the business entirely on your own. Building networks means letting key people know of your existence and giving them reason to tell others about you. The obvious people to tell are influential folks in your niche market. They can be your unpaid sales force. If you're getting ready to start a business selling computer and Internet services to seniors, it's good to interact with community leaders at the local "Sun City" or AARP chapter. Attend events in your target markets, and spread the word. Build affiliations and reciprocal agreements by placing your message with signs on the physical or electronic premises of others. It's good to let fringe competitors know of your existence. Don't think the local computer retailer will pitch you out on your ear when you start talking of

BUSINESS SUCCESS ESPECIALLY FOR SMALL BUSINESSES IS RELYING MORE AND MORE ON BUILDING EFFECTIVE NETWORKS.

services for seniors. They'd probably be glad to get rid of this challenging segment and send it in your direction. You'll be surprised what you may find when other business owners hear about your idea. True, some of this can be done after the business is started, but first-strike opportunity may be lost and you'll be too busy to create these kinds of networks once you're attending to daily operations.

Set Up Tracking Mechanisms

Setting up tracking mechanisms means establishing processes for collecting data that shows whether or not the business is successful. The basic thing you need for this is financial information—how much you sold and spent, in dollars. You'll need this for taxes. But lots of other information is out there to be collected to (1) tell you if you're successful and (2) improve your business effectiveness. This includes information on customers, who buys what, and the reasons why. Customer follow-up is important. This is critical in a niche business to ascertain viability and figure out if the niche is being served properly. Small shifts in product mix or even hours of operation can score big points with the niche. Collect as much transactional data as possible, talk to customers, and try doing a few well-crafted and intelligent surveys. This kind of data collection is too often left as a chore to be done after the business is started and so never gets done (not enough time) or gets lower priority ("I already know my business, why do I need to do that"). Such thinking is dangerous; it is always better to *prepare*.

Get the Message Ready

You have a new business. So what? It doesn't matter unless customers in your target niche know about it. This sounds obvious, but again, a little preparation can save a lot of turmoil later. Prepare a mix of launch advertising, publicity, trial offers, and other "hooks" to make target customers aware of your business and let them experience your product. This can be as simple as some of the things covered in the publicity chapter, like a newspaper story or a fire truck parked out in front of your new ice cream store. It can also include elaborately planned strategies like free samples and sales incentives for a sales force. A big "Coming Soon" sign is always effective, unless it's yet another outlet for your least-liked fast-food chain. What this means is taking a few key elements of the marketing plan and putting them actively to work shortly before the business itself starts.

Exit Strategy–Just in Case

You hope you'll never have to deal with this, but it can be good for sleep and family assurance to think through—in advance—how you'd exit the business if it *doesn't* work. This involves things like lease termination, product sellback, employee termination, and creditor payments. Having a palatable message ready is also a good idea; you don't want to alienate the niche completely since you may come back later with another idea. Many of the best laid business ideas fail in the market—perhaps the market was misread or isn't ready, or things just plain change. Having an exit strategy reduces risk for you and your supporters and avoids disasters that can stay with your "track record" for life. Exit strategy doesn't just mean

> HAVING AN EXIT STRATEGY REDUCES RISK FOR YOU AND YOUR SUPPORTERS AND AVOIDS DISASTERS THAT CAN STAY WITH YOUR "TRACK RECORD" FOR LIFE.

"quitting" the business; it can also cover significant shifts. If those seniors are simply too cheap to buy those computers from you, quit that part of the business and focus on services.

Go! It's Launch Day

Congratulations: You've prepared your plan and launch, and the big day is here. What happens on launch day will be obvious if you've completed the "ready" and "set" steps. Announcements, press releases, special offers, launch parties (with your customers, not just your employees and financial backers), and just plain talking to customers all play a key role in a successful launch. As you leave the starting blocks and begin to attain speed, it's important to talk to your customers. Find out if you're *really* meeting their needs. And watch the other runners to make sure someone else doesn't see your niche and move in a little too fast for your comfort. Figure out the threat and its magnitude. Develop a plan to stay ahead and keep your niche "captive." The best defense is sometimes offense, and vice versa.

The Longer Term

This chapter has focused on the critical stages of opening a niche business and covered the transition from researched ideas to real plans and successful implementation. The process certainly doesn't stop at the launch. All businesses evolve, no matter how "staid" they appear to be. New products, markets, efficiencies, and strategies constantly emerge. As a niche entrepreneur, you must continually adapt. The nice thing about niche marketing is that you don't have to react to competition since in a well defined niche, there shouldn't be so much. But as you know, that can change in a heartbeat. You have first-mover advantage, but your niche and its tastes can change, and other larger, more well-heeled competitors can move onto your "turf." The best advice is to keep your ideas and business plan open. The business plan is a "living document," always there to be updated for changing conditions or newly acquired knowledge. Such an attitude will probably be rewarding.

> THE BUSINESS PLAN IS A "LIVING DOCUMENT," ALWAYS TO BE UPDATED FOR CHANGING CONDITIONS AND NEWLY-ACQUIRED KNOWLEDGE.

One good entrepreneurial maxim is to develop the business in such a way as to eventually sell, or cash out of it. If your stated goal is always to create a saleable business that will fetch the best price, then everything that happens before and after launch is likely to be steered in a direction that creates business value, something tangible enough for someone else to see and pay for. Approaching your niche business in this way will be good for business. And a great many niche businesses *are* sold when larger companies serving neighboring niches and populations want to expand. If your niche becomes a trend, that expands the possibility even more.

Summary for Chapter 10

❖ Launching a business has "get ready," a "get set," and "go" stages.

❖ The "get ready" phase requires a business plan. This plan, which includes a marketing, operating, and financial plans, is especially important for a niche business. Without it, you may miss your niche, lose focus, and appear speculative and unproven to backers.

❖ Good business planning guides and templates are easy to find.

❖ The marketing plan defines the market—who it is, how big it is, and how your product or service will serve it.

❖ The operation plan maps out location, production, sourcing, and human resource strategies.

❖ The financial plan dollarizes the marketing and operating plans. Good financial plans articulate assumptions and project multiple scenarios.

❖ Business plans don't have to be perfect, just good. And they must be realistic.

❖ The "get set" stage is a coordinated preparation and execution of business plan elements. Acquiring and preparing resources, building networks, establishing tracking mechanisms, and identifying an exit strategy are all important parts of this stage.

❖ If all is done right in the "get ready" and "get set" stages, the "go" (launch) stage is easy. But don't forget to watch what happens at launch, and be prepared to adjust or modify the business and business plan. The business plan is an open, "living" document.

❖ Always think and act as though planning to sell the business.

This is going to take some work, but I bet it will be enlightening to think all this through. The marketing plan falls cleanly out of what I've developed reading Chapters 1-8. But now we're down to nuts and bolts—where to locate the evening center, how much it will cost, how to staff it, etc. Here's where my earlier idea about leasing a facility from an already existing day-care center needs to be checked out. And there might be a host of other alternatives, such as a gymnasium, or maybe a large unoccupied space owned by one of those restaurants that wants to get the parents out on Tuesdays. That old unused boxcar restaurant might be available cheap. And staff? Local college students have time in the evening and need money. Retirees and seniors from the local Sun City looking for something to do might like to handle the little ones and they also need money. I need to put all the ideas together with the dollars behind them. Still a go? Let's build a launch plan. Maybe I'll test the idea, start soliciting clients, and put up a few "coming soon" banners in strategic places. Boy am I going to be busy the next few months. I almost forgot—gotta be at work in half an hour...for another few weeks, anyway....

Go Forth
and Niche!

*W*hether or not I end up starting the evening care centers, this was sure an eye-opener! Never again will I think the same way about starting a business. My eyes will always be peeled for new niche opportunities and ways to expand upon the niches I've already discovered. I like to compete, but I like to win even more!

Regardless of economic climate, the United States is still the number-one place in the world to build a business, and it is *always* possible to go forth and seize control of your own financial destiny by building a profitable niche business. You have now read an entire book geared towards turning you into a niche idea generator and niche business entrepreneur. Instead of looking at the world around you as one that somehow excludes or prevents you from joining in the success, you now know how to read the radar, apply your skills, and capitalize on the opportunity.

The Niche Mentality

Never again will you pull into a crowded mall parking lot on a Saturday morning and curse the fact that you can't find a space; instead you will pull over and park your car anywhere you can and try to figure out just *what* brought all of those people there and *why*. You know the amount of infrastructure the business had to create, and the advertising the business had to buy to attract that crowd. Then you realize *you* can create something that will draw a good crowd too. A *better* crowd. A crowd that is part of your niche and loyal to your business almost regardless of price or advertising message. Don't forget: Undiscovered niches are everywhere, but you must open your eyes and thought processes to the possibilities.

You will begin to read the newspaper more closely, flip slowly and carefully through a magazine, listen intently to the evening news, and try to spot trends and shifts in the public's interest. Read those articles. Are you starting to see several a month on a particular topic? Hmmm...is there a potential business there? Read the ads. Is there a specific group of customers they target and hit? Or *miss*? Do you notice all your friends suddenly talking about something new and different? Is there a potential business *there*? Congratulations, you are a certified business idea machine. Don't let those ideas escape; *write them down*. Keep a notebook, an idea book, or a diary. Discuss ideas with your friends and family. Develop your ability to quickly assess markets and spot potential gaps. Ask yourself, What if.... What if there were a business built around preparing and delivering foods to allergy sensitive people? What if I could return a professional photograph anywhere, anytime to a client in two days? What if there were an *evening* child-care center? Chances are your first idea might not be your best. Stay tuned in, and keep at it.

> BE AN IDEA GENERATOR. KEEP A NOTEBOOK, AN IDEA BOOK, OR A DIARY. DISCUSS IDEAS WITH THE PEOPLE AROUND YOU. DEVELOP THE ABILITY TO QUICKLY ASSESS MARKETS AND SPOT POTENTIAL GAPS.

And never forget the enduring power of the niche concept. With such a business, you have a captive audience, and a captive *market*. This market was underserved before, or not served at all. Your customers or clients are probably *glad you're there* to serve their special need. They are loyal. They refer you to friends and associates who might have the same need. You got there first, and have little competition. You get the chance to serve the market on your own terms, unassailed and unaltered by the advertising budgets of well-heeled corporate competitors. You don't have to compete on price. Your customers *like* you, and you like them. Your niche may offer crossover opportunities to bring more products and services to your niche, or serve other niches with the same or similar product or service. There is little that's more satisfying to the entrepreneur, particularly the small one, than the niche scenario.

The Niche Opportunity

Creating a niche business is all about focusing on a market or a small subset of a market, specializing, and getting there first (if you can). If you can't get there first, is all hope lost? Not really. Don't forget that there's more to a product than the product itself. Remember that we pointed out the other ways to create a niche; it isn't just about the product, it can be about the service you provide around it. You can always create a specialty niche by modifying the following:

❖ *Delivery method and location.* Ask what the market needs when, and where it needs it. Is it in the store, at the front door, in the air, on the boat, poolside, or roomside?

❖ *Delivery speed.* Consider making it absolutely, positively overnight.

❖ *Packaging.* Think of the size (airline snacks) or style (customer's logo or design).

❖ *Price and value proposition.* Anyone fly Southwest Airlines?

Do you have a Chinese "Hot Wok" counter or similar co-located food service in your local grocery? There's probably nothing special about the food, but the owners have tinkered with the above variables to come up with a formula that works and gets them much farther ahead than if they had settled on starting an ordinary street corner Chinese restaurant.

By developing a niche business, you will be working towards a solid and secure future in which you can be

❖ *a bigger fish in a smaller pond.* You won't have to slug it out with competitors on every corner. You can find a market to own, and develop and maintain a comfortable and dominant position.

❖ *a frugal marketeer instead of a big bucks advertiser*. You will be able to get most of your exposure through word-of-mouth marketing, free publicity, and repeat customers.

❖ *in touch with market changes*. Because this is a niche you understand, you won't be caught off guard. You will stay in touch with the market and adapt quickly to what works and what doesn't. The minute a product stops selling, you will know. As soon as your customers need something new and ask you for it, you can adapt.

"Niching" Your Way In–and Out

Were you drawn to *Niche and Grow Rich* not because you have an idea for a niche business, but because you are just so darn unhappy with what you do now? This book should have helped you see that you have the power to recognize niches in the marketplace and capitalize on them. And what better place to focus than the industry in which you currently work? After all, you know it best.

Instead of focusing on your day to day unhappiness on the job, why not turn your energy towards using your ten-hour day as one big research project. The point of your new project is to ferret out the parts of your industry that could be improved (by you!) and modified (by you!), and where new products and services could easily be introduced (by you!). Instead of feeling the need to turn your back on what you do now and find something completely different in which to make a fresh start, you could be leveraging your deep knowledge and contacts into a valuable niche that only you can spot. You will feel invigorated by this new goal, and a sharper sense of purpose will fill your days. Get to the office early instead

> IF YOU'RE UNHAPPY WITH YOUR CURRENT JOB, USE THAT TEN-HOUR DAY AS ONE BIG RESEARCH PROJECT.

of late. This could be the day you stumble across that incredible idea.

This doesn't mean you should use this strategy to rebel and sabotage your long-standing relationship with your employer. Rather than breaking away and starting your own business, you might stumble onto something that hits it big for your company in the process. And you may get the rewarding chance to run it yourself! You can gain the experience and enjoy the success, *and then*, years later, look for a chance to do it yourself. Many new technology products start just this way—a niche is identified, a product is built, and the entrepreneur learns from the success and moves on with that or a similar product to start his or her own business. Anyone own a Palm Pilot?

Start Small and Build Experience

Does every business go straight from small seed to giant idea? No. You can start small and experiment, and each success will lead you towards a larger result. Jennifer's earliest experience with her regional women's business directory lead her to a slightly larger project with a national focus, *The Air Courier's Handbook*. With every small business success she published she learned more about the book and travel businesses and their niche markets, publicity, and the business fundamentals and profit margins of niche businesses. She ultimately learned enough about creating books and filling existing niche needs to create a "book packaging" and development business around that very notion. Yes, she often writes the books too, but the proverbial "golden goose" is in the creation of the ideas (you're reading one of them). And it isn't just the book, sometimes it's the distribution. Jennifer developed a specialty gift book called *The Cozy Book of Coffees and Cocoas* that manufacturers of espresso machines bought and bundled with their equipment. Perhaps you have a copy gathering dust on your kitchen shelf, right next to that Italian espresso machine you got for a wedding gift.

> YOU CAN START SMALL AND EXPERIMENT, AND EACH SUCCESS WILL LEAD TO A LARGER RESULT.

Your niche business idea can also start out small. You don't have to quit your job, mortgage your house, and risk everything. No, you can research, experiment, and test your ideas before growing them to the next stage. Nurture your ideas, refine your products, test them in the marketplace, and roll them out when and if you feel ready.

The Lure of Entrepreneurship

Who makes it big in America? Hard working entrepreneurs. You bought this book because you are interested in having a business of your own. That's why you read all ten chapters. But try to remember *why* you want a business of your own.

Several years ago the brokerage house Merrill Lynch decided to study their high-net-worth clients. The more they understood these folks, they thought, the more they'd be able to serve their needs. The company assumed they'd discover that their richest customers were from old families with inherited wealth. Isn't that what you would guess? In fact, what Merrill Lynch discovered was that 70 percent of their high-net-worth clients, the ones with assets of more than five million dollars, were wealthy because *they owned their own businesses*. They hadn't had the good fortune to be born to wealthy parents, and weren't highly paid executives with stock options, but had worked hard and saved and lived frugally. They were *entrepreneurs*. These folks had the same choices that you do—to work for someone else or for themselves. They chose to work for themselves and it paid off in a big, big way.

Wealth is seldom achieved by working for someone else. Starting a well-thought out niche business is usually a much better avenue. And people who start their own businesses not only make money, they also have fun doing it. You've probably sensed this in the countless examples shared in these pages. Running a business of your own is nerve-wracking, yes, but it is also a lot of fun! Remember John and Amy Drummond, the founders of Unicycle.com? Are they having more fun riding unicycles around town than they did when they worked for large corporations? You bet. Jalem Getz, the CEO of BuyCostumes.com vowed to wear a costume to work every day in the month of October as a way to get publicity for his Web site. Visitors could log on to the site every day and check to see what he was wearing that day. Is he having more

> WEALTH IS SELDOM ACHIEVED BY WORKING FOR SOMEONE ELSE.

fun running his own business than the poor businessman who has to show up every day wearing a suit and tie? Probably.

Contrast the flexibility and creativity you'd experience in running your own show with the rigidity and mind-numbing routine of working for someone else. Which sounds more appealing—taking orders from someone who owns the business you work for, or making decisions in your own business that will increase your profits? We've always chosen the latter, and think you will, too.

Focusing on the fun aspects of owning your own business might seem frivolous; what about the intellectual challenge? Do you ever feel like your brain isn't being fully utilized when working for someone else? It may seem like your true talents are undiscovered and your problem-solving skills are sleeping. This will not happen once you embark on the entrepreneurial journey. No entrepreneur has ever been bored. No entrepreneur has ever complained that their problem-solving skills are untapped. No entrepreneur has ever felt that success was too easy. Instead, the brave people who launch themselves into the unknown find they must draw upon every ounce of their creativity, inner strength, and resources in order to meet the challenges that arise every single day. Establish your own niche business, and you will instantly feel more alive. This sounds like a big claim, but ask any self-employed person and they will quickly agree.

Going Solo

It's natural to feel a certain anxiety about going out on your own. Will it work, and if it doesn't, who is there to help? It's like a solo hike up a large mountain; it's beautiful and exhilarating every step of the way, but what if you fall? Who's there to pick you up?

These visions dance in the head of every solo entrepreneur. But once they find a niche, suddenly—though it's still solo—the climb becomes a lot less steep and dangerous. The risks are still there, but they aren't preoccupying. Though there's no data to back this, it seems that the majority of "solo" entrepreneurs, whether it's conscious or subconscious, are serving a niche market. What may seem like (and is) common sense and good business practice to the entrepreneur, such as fast turnaround for professional photographs, defines a special, profitable, loyalty-building niche. It's one that can't or won't be easily duplicated by larger "generic" competitors.

Make Sure It's a *Viable* Niche

If there's one central message from earlier chapters, its that you should carefully assess and size the market. In Chapter 6 you learned the methods for identifying the viability and potential size of a market niche. The niche must be *definable, meaningful, sizeable,* and *reachable.* Once convinced the market is there, you must identify the need and the product or service that meets the need. Consider what the product is, what it isn't, and how it's different from other products already out there. Then, through a combination of data and creative listening, you assess the market and decide if it is really there, and if it is large enough to pursue.

Some of this analysis and appraisal is a bit like the marketing lessons you may have slugged through in business school, but it goes further. It is less "formula" and more about developing a creative common sense about a market. It involves thinking simultaneously "inside" and "outside" the box. True, it's a skill that some people don't have, but many more do than have been allowed to *use it* in the workplace. You still have to take a rational view, be realistic, look at the numbers, and stay somewhat on the conservative side. Webvan.com had a great niche, but overestimated its size and affinity for the product, which in turn rendered the accompanying operational innovations too expensive to sustain.

This business school "framework" material isn't nearly as much fun to read as the stories of successful entrepreneurs who have found their profitable niches. But don't cast it aside. Yes, it's good to be entrepreneurial, to take a leap of faith in your life and start your own business. But do it only *after* you have carefully examined the viability of your niche, the potential profitability, and the long term prospects for success. To use an old carpenter's adage, "measure twice, cut once." Probe and measure that market again and again before you take steps to invest your money. Make a test cut or two, and be sure (1) the wood is sound and (2) you don't spoil good wood.

> TO USE AN OLD CARPENTER'S ADAGE, "MEASURE TWICE, CUT ONCE." PROBE AND MEASURE THAT MARKET AGAIN AND AGAIN BEFORE INVESTING MONEY. MAKE A TEST CUT OR TWO TO MEASURE YOUR BUSINESS IDEA ON A SMALL SCALE.

Business books can be deadly dull, and we hope you have found *Niche and Grow Rich* to be a lively companion. It should have encouraged you to take bold and imaginative steps when thinking about business and new ways to develop ideas for profitable businesses, to reach out and identify customers, and to get your message out to the right audience. (And if you already have your own business, this book and its concepts are for you, too. Redirect towards those niches, and become even more successful.) The hope is that it has emboldened you to dream and plan and move towards finding the business that is right for you. And that its sage advice will accompany you on your journey from the first tentative steps through triumphant entry onto the marketplace.

Remember, you are not alone in your dreams. Every business giant you now idolize, from Ray Kroc of McDonald's, to Jeff Bezos of Amazon.com to Howard Schultz of Starbucks, was once in your same position. They too had a dream, and they researched, planned, and began to take small step after small step to turn that dream into a solid business reality. Years from now, we could be reading about YOU and your thriving niche empire. Get started today, and your future success will be one day closer.

Resources

Books

Business Planning and Development

Abrams, Rhonda *The Successful Business Plan*, Running "R" Media, Palo Alto, CA, 2000

Parmerlee, David, *Preparing the Marketing Plan*, NTC Business Books, Chicago, 2000

Hendricks, Mark and John Riddle, *Business Plans Made Easy*, Entrepreneur Press, Irvine, CA, 2002

Bygrave, William D., editor, *The Portable MBA in Entrepreneurship, 2nd edition*, John Wiley & Sons, New York, 1997

Rohr, Ellen, *How Much Should I Charge?*, Max Rohr, Inc., 1999

Marketing and Business Ideas

Moore, Geoffrey and McKenna, Regis, *Crossing the Chasm—Marketing and Selling High Tech Products to Mainstream Customers*, 2nd edition, HarperBusiness, New York, 1999

Hall, Doug, *Jump Start Your Business Brain*, Brain-Brew Books, Cincinnati, OH, 2001

Kawasaki, Guy, *Rules for Revolutionaries: The Capitalist Manifesto for Creating and Marketing New Products and Services*, Harperbusiness, New York, 2000

Kawasaki, Guy, *Selling the Dream: How to Promote Your Product, Company, or Ideas—And Make a Difference—Using Everyday Evangelism*, Harperbusiness, New York, 1992

Smith, Ellen Reid, *e-Loyalty: How to Keep Customers Coming Back to Your Website*, Harperbusiness, New York, 2000

Periodicals

American Demographics, Media Central/Primedia, New York

The Wall Street Journal, Dow Jones & Co., New York

The New York Times, New York Times Co., New York

USA Today, Gannett Media, Washington, DC

Entrepreneur Magazine, Irvine, CA

Fortune Small Business, Time Inc., New York

Web Sites
General Business, Marketing, Entrepreneurship

Entrepreneur.com (www.entrepreneur.com), including bookstore www.smallbizbooks.com

Small Business Administration (www.sba.gov)

Netscape Netbusiness (netbusiness.netscape.com)

Search Engines

Yahoo! (www.yahoo.com)

Google (www.google.com)

Dogpile (www.dogpile.com)

Northern Light (www.northernlight.com)

LexisNexis (www.lexisnexis.com)

Market Data and Data Services

U.S. Census (www.census.gov)

Claritas (www.claritas.com) and Claritas Express (www.claritasexpress.com)

Demographics Now (www.demographicsnow.com)

USADATA (www.usadata.com)

Franchising

Entrepreneur Franchise Zone (www.entrepreneur.com/franchise_zone)

International Franchise Association (www.franchise.org)

Franchising.org (www.franchising.org)

American Association of Franchisees and Dealers (www.aafd.org)

Intellectual Property

Entrepreneur.com (www.entrepreneur.com)

U.S. Patent and Trademark Office (www.uspto.gov)

Publicity and Publicity Skills

PublicityHound (www.publicityhound.com)

PRSecrets (www.prsecrets.com)

Toastmasters (www.toastmasters.org)

Index